Padre Pio Gleanings

Pascal Cataneo

Translated by
Maureen McCollum
and Gabriel Dextraze

Éditions Paulines

This book originally appeared as: *I Fioretti di Padre Pio*, Edizioni Dehoniane, Rome, 1988.

Statement

Phototypesetting: *Éditions Paulines*

Cover: *Jean-Pierre Normand*

ISBN 2-89039-507-3

Legal deposit — 3rd quarter 1991
Bibliothèque nationale du Québec
National Library of Canada

© 1991 Éditions Paulines
       250, boul. Saint-François Nord
       Sherbrooke, QC, J1E 2B9

CONTENTS

FOREWORD

I am privileged to have known Padre Pio personally. My first meeting with him took place at midday on June 17th, 1940. I had just arrived from Bologna where, the day before, I had been ordained priest. I reached San Giovanni Rotondo which was then quite different from the small city it has since become. Before going to my own native village on Mount Gargano, I visited Padre Pio to consult him on a few personal spiritual problems to find out what he felt and to get his advice on them. I wanted to make a good start as a priest right from the very beginning.

Padre Pio received me in his cell, telling me he had not been able to go down to the chapel that day because of a severe headache. He immediately kissed my hands, as I was a new priest, and made himself completely available to me for as long as I wanted. At the end, he told me what he felt and gave me his advice.

To be honest, on walking out of his cell, I had the impression that he had not given me more than any other priest I might have consulted. At that time I was also under the illusion that he had a kind of miraculous solution for every problem presented to him. With time, however, I learned that Padre Pio intervened in a special way only when God moved him in that direction.

As a matter of fact, in all the years I knew and met with him, from 1940 to his death in 1968, I experienced extraordinary interventions on very few, rare occasions. It is mostly through other people, intimately connected with him, and through the numerous biographies written on him, that I have put together what is recorded here.

In this way I have become aware of the many sides of his personality harmoniously blended into a deep humanity and profound spirituality which spontaneously manifested itself in many circumstances. I want to show this through this variety of episodes which I call: *I Fioretti di Padre Pio* (Padre Pio Gleanings) not because they have entered into the realm of legend, but because they have an aura of mystery surrounding them.

Twenty years after his death, the picture of Padre Pio, far from fading, has taken on the dimensions and bearing of a giant in faith. One day, when a Brother remarked that the large number of visitors attracted by him meant a great deal of extra work for those around him, Padre Pio replied prophetically: "This is nothing to what it will be one day!" On another occasion he said: "Wait a while... and you will see how truth will fly at you." We now see the fulfilment of those words. My desire is to contribute in some small way to a better understanding of Padre Pio by offering these "gleanings" for our reflection. I believe that what is written here, presented in a style acceptable to our contemporaries, will help build up that Kingdom of God so much needed by our world.

Naples, 03-29-88   *Pascal Cataneo*

1

A POWERFUL VISION

To understand better what motivated Padre Pio throughout his life, we must keep in mind a very special vision he had in 1902. He later spoke of this significant event to his confessor, in the third person singular, using his baptismal name.

"A man of majestic appearance and rare beauty, shining like the sun, stood beside Francis and took him by the hand. After reassuring him he gave Francis this invitation: "Come with me for you must fight like a valiant warrior." Francis was led to a vast countryside, through a multitude of men divided into two groups. On one side were very handsome men dressed in robes which were as white as snow. On the other side were very ugly men dressed in black robes and who appeared to be more like dark shadows.

The young man, standing between these two groups, saw a giant creature coming towards him. His forehead touched the clouds and he had horrible features.

The mysterious person in the shining white robes standing at his side told Francis to fight the monster. Francis begged to be spared from the fury of this strange being but was told: "You cannot escape this. You must fight. Courage! Go, fight boldly and with confidence. I will be here beside you to help you and I will not allow the creature to defeat you.

The battle began and it was terrible. Helped by the resplendent person in white, Francis had the upper hand. The monster was forced to retreat followed by all the ugly, shadowy men, shouting, screaming and cursing at the top of their voices. The handsome group in white robes applauded and praised the one who had helped Francis in this hard battle.

The resplendent one, who shone brighter than the sun, placed an indescribably beautiful crown on Francis' head but removed it immediately saying: "Another crown, more beautiful than this, will be yours if you learn to fight this creature you have just defeated. He will always be back to attack you. Fight bravely and count on my help. Don't be afraid of being harassed by him nor terrified by his terrible appearance. I will be with you and I will help you every time so that you will be victorious over him."

Padre Pio was called, in an extraordinary way, to wage war against the forces of evil, against those who assail mankind, against those who direct these forces and represent them, to help build up the Kingdom of God.

This struggle would be enacted, directly or indirectly, a thousand and one time, in various ways. The events reported in these pages offer only a few examples. They are, however, numerous enough to amaze us. May they also inspire us to advance on the path of spiritual maturity, to the point of finding perfection in the fullness of Christ!

2

A SEPTEMBER MORNING, 1918

Padre Pio received the stigmata, or Wounds of Christ, on September 20th, 1918. This event determined his destiny and made of him a powerful sign to the world. What does this phenomenon mean? It probably parallels what St. Paul said of himself when he wrote: "I am suffering now... in my own flesh to complete what is lacking in the sufferings of Christ." (Col. 1:24) What is lacking in Christ's suffering? Absolutely nothing! His sufferings have an infinite value and redeem the whole world without any extra help from us. If something is lacking it is because God decides it is lacking, and this is humanity's free participation in its own redemption. Here we have to understand the Christian meaning of sin as the rejection of God's love. In sin, we have what St. Augustine calls: "A love of creatures to the point of contempt for God." This is a love which goes beyond the law of God and brings a pleasure that separates us from God. God is loved by detaching oneself from the inordinate love of creatures. This detachment is as painful as setting a dislocated bone, only here we are speaking of love. It is not a matter of accepting suffering for the sake of suffering. This is neither human nor even Christian, but suffering is an essential component of love.

Padre Pio's stigmata caused him continual and intense suffering. The Lord asked from him an extraordinary participation to "complete what is lacking in the sufferings of Christ." (Col. 1:24) He accepted with all his heart whatever God asked of him. Sometimes, when asked by his spiritual sons about the suffering the stigmata caused him, he lifted the veil a little to reveal a sight terrifying to anyone.

He particularly spoke of what he endured while celebrating Mass during which, in some degree, he lived again the Passion of Christ. However, when others offered to share his terrible agony, Padre Pio would tell them he was jealous of his sufferings and that he would not give them up to anyone! This showed his great love of God and for souls. He not only accepted his suffering but desired it to save the numberless sinners who crowded around him.

The Event

No one actually saw Padre Pio receive the stigmata. On that day, Father Paolino da Casacalenda, his Superior, was at San Marco in Lamis, a village near San Giovanni Rotondo, and the other members of the community were out. Everything took place between Padre Pio and the Lord, in deepest intimacy, before the crucifix which is still to be seen in the tribune above the entrance to the little church.

Padre Pio did not want this occurrence to become known but the time came when his Provincial

Superior, Father Benedetto, from San Marco in Lamis insisted that he write down an account of the incident. On October 22nd, 1918, Padre Pio agreed and wrote the following:

"On the 20th of last month, in the tribune after the celebration of Mass, I was overcome by a state of repose like a deep and peaceful sleep. All my senses, interior and exterior, as well as the faculties of my soul were plunged into an indescribable stillness. In addition, there was a total silence within me and around me followed by a deep peace. Then, in a flash, I saw before me someone like the mysterious person I had seen on August 5th, but with one difference: his hands, feet and side were running with blood..."

Padre Pio was in great distress and deeply distraught. Engulfed in pain he could not rise from the floor and had to crawl, on all fours, back to his cell leaving a trail of blood in the corridor. He tried to wipe away the blood as best he could and then hid the wounds with bandages.

On returning to the monastery, Father Paolino, the Superior, noticed that Padre Pio was behaving rather strangely but did not give this a second thought. Gradually, he began to sense that Padre Pio was hiding something from him. He questioned him but Padre Pio gave nothing away. Somehow, he heard talk of stigmata. He was suspicious and wanted to get to the bottom of things. One day he walked into Padre Pio's cell without knocking on the door and discovered the secret. He immediately informed the Provincial Superior who urged the greatest prudence on the matter and asked Padre Pio to write down all that had happened to him. From that moment a strongly emotional atmosphere surrounded the Padre, which ranged from a cult to violent aversion! This would be his Calvary. Until the day he died Padre Pio would be a sign of contradiction.

"Hey! What are you doing?"

At the beginning, Padre Pio took great care to hide his wounds, not only from visitors but from his brothers in religion. One of them, who was quite close to him, noticed that the priest was so completely taken up with the sufferings he bore for the love of Christ and the salvation of souls, that he had not changed his socks for a longtime. One day, when Padre Pio was ill, this young Brother who was looking after him suggested that it might be good to have his feet washed. Padre Pio let him do it. His confrère was able to see for himself that his feet were covered with scabs which made it difficult for him to walk. The Brother scraped them off with great care, washed and dried his feet, and then kissed them before putting on his sandals. At this Padre Pio called out: "Hey! What are you doing?" The brother explained that this was the custom whenever he washed anyone's feet. "Well! said Padre Pio, "You can do that to other people but not to me!"

Capuchin versus Benedictine

Padre Pio had been suffering for a long time from a severe hernia which caused him pain and difficulty in walking. He had always avoided having an operation until the day he could stand it no longer and consulted a surgeon. The doctor, Giorgio Festa, was one of his converts and very devoted to him. A room in the monastery was prepared for the operation on October 10th, 1925. When the moment came to put the patient under anaesthesia he refused and said: "Will you be able to resist looking at my wounds?" The doctor replied: "No!" with great frankness. "Now you see why I cannot allow myself to be put to sleep!" said Padre Pio. The surgeon pointed out that the operation would be long and painful but Padre Pio had been ordered, by his provincial, to hide his stigmata and he wanted to obey even at the price of such suffering. He refused the anaesthesia. Doctor Festa asked him to drink at least a little Benedictine to sustain him. He took some and when the doctor offered a second glass Padre Pio cut him short saying: "No! That's quite enough, otherwise there will be fisticuffs between the Capuchin and the Benedictine!" The operation was performed and, as expected, was very painful. Padre Pio endured the suffering with superhuman strength. In the end he fainted as he was being taken to his cell. Doctor Festa took advantage of this situation to hurriedly examine the stigmata in the presence of two of the Brothers and so got what he wanted in spite of Padre Pio's protests.

3

FROM FAR AND WIDE

People flocked to Padre Pio. Generally, they were men and women who wanted to leave behind a life of sin. He led them to God. His methods of conversion were matter for discussion. Padre Pio could be quite blunt and even, at times, violent; this was rather misleading. There were profound reasons for this behaviour. It was pointed out to him that his harshness was rather disconcerting and could distance souls from him. He replied: "I treat souls as God wants me to treat them." And there were those God indicated to him who needed to be shaken up otherwise they would not give up their evil ways. We know that some illnesses can be treated with medicine while others need surgery. We generally turn to surgery when medication fails. I think Padre Pio could be considered as a "surgeon of souls". When he was hard on someone, that man or woman might well be annoyed and even resentful but if the desire for conversion was genuine he or she would come back to Padre Pio. This way of acting was not a vent for his anger but a tactic for saving souls.

About six weeks after Padre Pio's death I went to pray at his grave. At that time I wanted to meet with Father Pellegrino Funicelli who had assisted him in his last moments. I asked him about Padre Pio's brusqueness and he told me he had personally witnessed one of these outbursts. It concerned a woman at the monastery door. As soon as the door was closed and Padre Pio had gone inside, he became calm and serene, as if nothing had happened. He pointed out to me that normal anger, generally, does not die down so quickly.

There were other reasons for this harsh behaviour. Padre Pio, who was more clearly aware than anyone of his position of creature towards God, could not stand the veneration and fanatical outpourings directed at him by so many people and he was driven to react violently against this attitude. However, it has to be said that beneath this rough exterior lay a very tender and sensitive heart. He was probably trying to protect himself from the weakness of his own human nature. This type of conduct, on his part, has to be prudently considered for what it is worth.

Beniamino Gigli in trouble

In a popular magazine, the mother of the famous Italian tenor, Beniamino Gigli, told the story of her son's first meeting with Padre Pio. The tenor wanted to meet the priest after he had heard various stories from friends about the extraordinary things he did. He arrived at San Giovanni Rotondo in a luxurious car with a uniformed chauffeur and aroused a great deal of curiosity. At this time he had already established an international reputation.

When Gigli was introduced to Padre Pio, the priest gave him that searching look of his which went to the heart of things without being influenced by appearances. He went up to him and attacked him point blank with: "You call yourself 'Gigli', like the lily which is a symbol of purity but you are a sullied lily because you are cheating on your wife and have a secret relationship with another woman. You call yourself "Beniamino" which means beloved of God but God does not love you at all because of the state of your soul." One can imagine how upset the tenor was on hearing this. Padre Pio had read in his soul what others chose to ignore and had confronted him with his responsibility. Beniamino, however, had the strength and humility to accept the brutal indictment. He changed his ways, broke off his extra-marital relationship and, until his death he was a faithful friend of the priest. In his later years he often visited Padre Pio for advice and comfort.

Padre Pio was always very happy to see him and often asked him to sing his best known song "Mamma" because it made him think back, with great tenderness, on his own mother, Peppa. More often than not Padre Pio did not hear it to the end because it moved him so much he went away to cry.

"Go back to 1936!"

The comedian, Carlo Campanini, who is buried in the San Giovanni Rotondo cemetery, first met Padre Pio in 1939 but it took another eleven years before he really changed his life for the better.

His first meeting with the priest was not motivated by anything religious but, quite simply, for material benefit. The actor was constantly on the road and away from his family who lived in Rome. He was rather unhappy about this and wanted work that would bring him closer to home. One day a colleague told him about a cousin who had sorted out some family problems, thanks to the good offices of Padre Pio. Carlo wanted a similar favour. At one point he was in Bari and took advantage of this to go on to San Giovanni accompanied by a friend who would introduce him to Padre Pio.

It was Holy Week and the priest was more than ever lost in deep meditation on the Passion of Christ. The two friends arrived late and got into the monastery only after a great deal of persistence! When he saw them, Padre Pio exclaimed: "Even during Holy Week they won't give me any peace! What do you want?" Campanini and his friends answered that they wanted to go to confession. Padre Pio said to them: "Go and make your preparation in the church. I will hear your confession after Mass tomorrow. They went away and returned next morning as agreed. Campanini was very moved by Padre Pio's Mass. He thought it would never end, all the more so since he was kneeling in a very awkward position. The Mass over, he went to confession and was taken aback to hear the priest cite his sins one by one. Before giving absolution Padre Pio made him promise to change his life. Campanini really wanted to speak about his real reason for coming, that is to find work in Rome so as to be near his family, but he did not have the courage to do so. However, he made his request interiorly, from the depth of his heart, with much insistence.

Back in Rome, he was unexpectedly called to Cinecittà to read for an important role in the film *"Addio Giovinezza"* (Goodbye Youth). The candidates for the part included many actors much better known than Campanini but he was the one chosen. This opened up for him a career which made him rich and famous. He had parts in over a hundred other films in quick succession! By the end of 1949 he had reached the height of his success and wealth. But he had not kept the promise made to Padre Pio about changing his life and this troubled him.

One day his wife announced to him that she wanted to consecrate the family to the Sacred Heart. She had spoken of it to the pastor in their parish and he had suggested that for such an occasion it would be good that she and her husband go to confession and Holy Communion. Campanini did not dare go against his wife's wishes and told her he would give it some thought. The consecration was fixed for January 8th, 1950. Two days before, on the feast of the Epiphany, Campanini was walking in Rome when he happened to pass by a church. He went in with the intention of going to confession but when he saw the priest, who was a very large, fat man, he changed his mind. Looking around he saw another priest, who was slightly built, praying before a crucifix. Soon he got up, went to the confessional to take over from the other priest. He had hardly sat down when he called Campanini over and offered to hear his confession. The comedian agreed and was quite radiant when he left the church because he realized that he could now go back to

Padre Pio without having to confess all the sins he had committed up until that time and so Padre Pio would be unaware that he had not kept his promise! As arranged, the consecration took place in his home. Later he took advantage of an opportunity offered and went to visit Padre Pio expecting that he could make an "ordinary" confession to him. However the priest, who cared about him and had his protection at heart, wanted him to wipe his soul clean and said to him: "Begin from 1936!" Campanini tried to convince him that it had not been that long since his last confession, but in vain. Padre Pio was quite inflexible: "Begin from 1936!" Campanini did as he was told and from that time he and Padre Pio forged a very strong spiritual bond and a deep friendship which lasted until the comedian's death.

"Why are you here with us?"

One of the conversions brought about by Padre Pio resulted in a chain reaction. It was that of the lawyer Cesare Festa, an avowed and prominent Freemason, cousin of Padre Pio's personal doctor Giorgio Festa. One day Giorgio challenged his cousin to visit Padre Pio and see for himself the supernatural powers he denounced so much. The lawyer accepted the challenge and went to San Giovanni Rotondo. Padre Pio was talking with some people when he noticed Cesare Festa. Immediately he left the group and confronted him with: "Well! Why are you here with us? You are a prominent Freemason." The lawyer agreed. Padre Pio then asked: "What is the duty of freemasonry?" He replied: "To overthrow the Church."

After this preamble, which no one had expected, Padre Pio changed, took the lawyer by the hand and invited him to follow him. He told the story of the Prodigal Son, very simply and very effectively. Suddenly Cesare identified with the young man and, even more, began to feel very strongly the love God has for those who stray from him. He gave in, went to confession and when he got up from his knees he had the impression that he had been born again into a new kind of life. Some days later he went back to Padre Pio who wrote these words for him on the title page of a New Testament: "Blessed are those who listen to the word of God, guard it jealously and accomplish it faithfully." This was a warning and an exhortation to be rooted in his new state of grace. The lawyer understood and welcomed this and resolved to remain in this new way of life.

One day he decided to go on a pilgrimage to Lourdes. When the Freemasons' Lodge in Genoa heard this, they became alarmed at the possible consequences of such a conversion. They called a meeting to solemnly condemn this turncoat. In no way intimidated, Cesare Festa decided to attend the meeting. As he was leaving, someone brought him a letter from Padre Pio encouraging him not to be ashamed of his faith and to fight: "The Lord will help you." At the meeting, the former Freemason explained his conversion and rigorously defended the Church. After this he became a fervent Christian and a devout follower of Padre Pio.

"Oh! Man from Genoa, you are close to the sea but you do not know how to wash yourself!"

Among the chain of conversions brought on by that of the lawyer Cesare Festa, was that of Doctor Ezio Saltamerenda, Director of the Institute of Biotherapy in Genoa. A convinced atheist from youth he took every possible occasion to advance his ideas. On hearing of Doctor Festa's conversion he wanted to see this Padre Pio for himself so he set out for San Giovanni Rotondo. Padre Pio had never seen this man before but he noticed him in the crowd and addressed him personally saying: "Oh! Man from Genoa, you are close to the sea but you do not know how to wash yourself!" Saltamerenda was shaken to his roots by this soul-analysis. How was this priest able to identify him and depict his soul with such precision? Could it be that the supernatural, which he had so long denied, really did exist after all? He began to see that he had to wash his soul of its stains just as he washed his body. Overcome by revulsion from his spiritual state, which had been revealed to him so suddenly, he wanted to confess his sins to Padre Pio. The priest knew that he was not ready to confess and that his soul was not lucid enough to benefit from the grace of God. Padre Pio refused. Aware of his condition, Saltamerenda was very ill at ease. His soul was disturbed, his mind in a quandary when, suddenly, a very strange thing happened to him. He noticed a strong scent of violets surrounding him. Brother Francis came across him in this state of extreme anxiety. When the doctor explained the reason for his crisis the Brother took him by the hand back to the cell of Padre Pio whose tactics he knew very well! As soon as the door opened the scent of violets again wafted around Saltamerenda. This time, Padre Pio welcomed him with kindness and during confession the priest listed one by one all the sins the doctor had committed since childhood and then gave him absolution. From this moment on, Saltamerenda became a devoted follower of Padre Pio and with the same enthusiasm he had shown for spreading his atheistic ideas, he now set out to make Padre Pio known.

The perfumed poster

The internationally acclaimed sculptor, Francesco Messina, had been brought up without any religious instruction whatsoever and, as an adult, was far from being a practising Catholic. A pragmatist by nature, he had no time for stories of miracles. In the spring of 1945 he organized an exhibition of his work in Genoa. This was advertised on posters throughout the city. One evening he and his wife went to dinner with friends who were very devoted to Padre Pio. They talked at length about the Capuchin of Gargano and showed him a thick biography of the priest. Messina leafed through it and was particularly struck by Padre Pio's penetrating eyes in one of his photographs.

After dinner he and his wife went back to their hotel but he could not sleep because of the effect of those penetrating eyes. Around five o'clock in the morning he was aroused from his sleep by the telephone. Who could it be? What news could justify such an early call? As it was so early and because he did not get much sleep Messina was in a foul mood when he answered. His irritation grew when he heard the voice of a childhood friend who told him that he had smelled the perfume of Padre Pio coming from a poster, advertising his exhibition in Place De Ferrari. His friend went on to say that this "coincidence" could be explained. The perfume was calling Messina to go immediately to Padre Pio. His friend on the telephone was Saltamerenda, and he insisted! Messina was about to tell him "to go to hell" but he controlled himself. Instead he told his insistent friend that he would think about it and excused himself by saying he had important work to do in Milan.

He did, in fact, leave for Milan but the thought of Padre Pio would not leave him. Finally, he decided that he really had to meet this man. A short time later he contacted Saltamerenda and together they went to San Giovanni Rotondo. It was late when they arrived at the monastery and Padre Pio had already retired to his cell. Saltamerenda insisted on going in and because the community knew him well he got his way. Padre Pio was a bit cross with Saltamerenda and turned to Messina saying: "And what do you want?" Messina replied that for a long time he had wanted to meet him and now that he had done so he wanted to place himself in his hands. Padre Pio replied rather abruptly: "You certainly are in good hands!" He told them to go to the church and prepare for confession and he would come down later to hear them. Messina wanted to say that he did not feel psychologically or spiritually ready for confession but the priest had already walked away. When he came down to the church later the sculptor hastened to tell the priest that he was not at all ready. Padre Pio stopped him in his tracks: "Listen, just say nothing and answer me." He then began a detailed review of all Messina's sins from childhood until that moment. Messina paled and then surrendered when faced with this kind of spiritual projector which pitilessly unfolded before him all the tortuous ways of his soul. Next day he attended at Padre Pio's Mass and went to Holy Communion. His life changed radically. He became one of Padre Pio's most faithful spiritual sons. He used to say: "I was born on April 11th, 1949." This was the day he had met Padre Pio. Until the priest's death, Messina visited him frequently and sculpted the monumental Way of the Cross which can be seen today on the way up the hill near the Church of S. Maria delle Grazie at San Giovanni Rotondo.

"That is heresy!"

The case of Frederic Abresch is seen as a milestone in the list of conversions attributed to Padre Pio. This man, German by origin, had turned from Protestantism to Catholicism, not by conviction but for convenience. He went in for studies of the occult which gave him no peace and would now and then come to church only under sufferance because his wife was a devout Catholic and a follower of Padre Pio.

Urged by his wife, Frederic Abresch went one day to San Giovanni Rotondo to meet this priest who did such extraordinary things. His first meeting took place in December, 1928. He was quite indifferent at first until he went to confession. Padre Pio told him that in previous confessions he had held back grave sins and asked him if he was really serious about confessing. Abresch tried to justify the matter by explaining that he considered confession as a useful convention but could not accept that it was supernatural. Padre Pio's expression became extremely stern and sad and he cried out: "That is heresy!" Then he told Abresch that all his communions had been sacrilegious and that he had to start again from zero! The man would have to prepare himself by going back to his last "good" confession. Padre Pio then went off to hear women's confessions. Abresch was devastated and could not recall his past to mind.

When the priest returned to the sacristy, the poor man was still in a state of utter bewilderment. Padre Pio then took the initiative and by careful questioning paraded his whole life before him and finished by saying: "You have been singing a hymn to Satan while Jesus, in his divine love, has been breaking his neck for you!" After this crystal-clear reading of his soul Abresch felt a deep sense of repentance. When he left the confessional, pardoned, he felt rejuvenated and filled with unspeakable joy. Things did not stop there. His wife who had first encouraged her husband to meet Padre Pio, found herself in a very painful situation. Doctors had advised an operation with side effects that would prevent her from having children. She ardently desired to be a mother. Abresch asked Padre Pio's advice. After having prayed, the priest said: "No operation!" From that moment his wife felt completely cured. Two years later Padre Pio predicted that Abresch and his wife would have a son who would become a priest one day. This prediction was fulfilled.

Nair: The red "Passionaria" of Emilia

There was a woman in Bologna who was one of those people who when they take up a cause give themselves completely to it. For her it was all or nothing! Her name was Italia Betti but she was known as Naïr. Her cause was the struggle for human justice. She firmly believed from the outset that this battle could only be won by Communism.

Born into a poor family of thirteen children, she had had to make enormous sacrifices to get her doctorate and become a teacher of mathematics and physics at the Galvani High School in Bologna. As a member of the Communist Party she became a fervent militant. Her commitment had a kind of religious charism about it. After many years on this road she became weary, physically and morally, because she began to realize that Communism did not have the solutions to the cause she had given her life to, that of justice. During this period she had a dream about Padre Pio. He stood beside a house which brought terror to anyone who went inside. The choice was offered, either to go into the house in terror or remain outside in peace. She was impressed by this dream and wanted to solve the puzzle. She decided to go and speak with Padre Pio in person. She went to San Giovanni Rotondo with her mother and sister on December 14th, 1949. They attended Padre Pio's Mass and this celebration opened up such spiritual dimensions for her that she felt compelled to reflect on them. She spent a good two hours in the church. When, afterwards, she went to Padre Pio for confession, she understood that the struggle for true justice can only be realized within the context of a Christian view of life. She became a convert and expended all her energies on the spiritual path indicated by the priest. She no longer wanted to leave San Giovanni. Leaving all she had in Bologna, she had a small house built near the man who had converted her. She died on the October 26th, 1950. In her last will and testament she wrote:

> "My return to the Church, after I had rejected it for twenty years, was done knowingly and not simply through fear of losing my life. It was the result of my conscience crying out for peace. It did not take long for me to come to the profound understanding that life was not what I had been living until that time. I understood also, in an indisputable way, that it was absurd to think of men — those little organized molecules of the universe — as the coordinators of all the human sciences. Man is a divine creation so he must feel part of it all and not be an end in himself. He must recognize that he is only a little particle of energy which constantly needs a guide to help him go on."

"That's quite enough!"

Giovanni Bardazzi, a good Tuscan, was not lacking in ardour or daring. He had joined the ranks of the Communist Party in Prato and had been put in charge of a branch. His one aim was to restore order according to the Communist ideology. He could not bear the sight of priests, monks or nuns. One day he found some Sisters in his house. He threw them out and turned on his wife who had let them in. He wanted all the churches turned into dance halls and worked at this like a madman. One night, in a dream, he saw a bearded friar, his hands in mittens, who said to him: "That's quite enough! It's time to stop all this! I am waiting for you at San Giovanni Rotondo." Bardazzi was very disturbed by this dream. Who could this religious be? Where is San Giovanni Rotondo? He spoke to his wife who not only told him who the friar was and where he could find San Giovanni Rotondo but encouraged him to go there and clear up what was going on in his mind. He was hesitant: "Will I go or won't I?" After some time he decided he had to get to the bottom of it all and set out for San Giovanni Rotondo with his wife and some friends.

On arriving, he sent his wife and friends off to the monastery while he sought out the local Communist Party headquarters. He had no doubt they would fill him in on this hoaxer. To his utter amazement his comrades were far from sharing his views on the priest. No one meddled with Padre Pio! Bardazzi could not understand and labelled them lukewarm Communists. The only thing to do was to go to the monastery and check this man out for himself. When he got there another surprise lay in store. A crowd waited to get into the church, praying as they waited, with rosaries in hand, even the men! He understood less and less. What kind of world was this?

He told himself he would talk to this priest next day and "put him straight". He was convinced that all this was a hoax to deceive poor people. Maybe, but he would not be taken in by it! Padre Pio arrived and Bardazzi went forward and started to tremble all over! What the devil was going on? On reaching him Padre Pio said very quietly: "The black sheep has returned". "Good God! Some compliment!" thought Bardazzi. The poor man suddenly found himself engulfed in a strange atmosphere and heading for a very disturbing spiritual crisis.

The next day he went to Padre Pio's Mass then celebrated at the altar of St. Francis in the old chapel. Bardazzi placed himself so that he could see every move of Padre Pio. When the friar turned round and extended his arms at the "Pray brethren..." his hands were bare and the stigmata, surrounded by blood, could be clearly seen. Everyone present was astounded and deadly silent because of the suffering they saw on the priest's face. Bardazzi wanted proof. "If it is true that this priest suffers the Passion of Christ at this moment why couldn't he, Bardazzi, have some share of it too?" What a thought! Suddenly, an intolerable pain seized him. It lasted only an instant but it seemed like an eternity to Bardazzi. This is how the fiery, hot-headed Tuscan was introduced to the supernatural ambience surrounding Padre Pio. He was perplexed by it. He saw things in a different light, the light of grace, and became aware of his own sinfulness. He wanted to go to confession but Padre Pio asked him: "Tell me, what has the Lord done to you?" Bardazzi replied: "Nothing! I don't even know if he exists." "What do you mean, you don't know if he exists? Of course he exists!" The two men entered into a serious dialogue that led nowhere. For Padre Pio this man was not ready and he told him in no uncertain terms: "I cannot give you absolution because I don't want to go to hell because of you!" Bardazzi was plunged in the deepest darkness of spirit. He racked his brains, questioned his conscience and decided to get out of this mess, enlightened and convinced. Little by little, with the help of God's grace and Padre Pio's prayers light began to flood his soul. He saw himself with the eyes of Christ and sincerely asked forgiveness. Then he went to Padre Pio who gave him absolution. A totally transformed Bardazzi returned to Prato. He left the Communist Party and endured the taunts of his former comrades. He showed the strength of soul and spiritual certitude which was his, with the help of Padre Pio, and began a new life.

A slow conversion

Conversion is not always an instant affair. Sometimes it comes in stages and adapts to the state of the soul which needs to move slowly to assimilate the truths of faith, one by one. One such person was Alberto del Fante. He was a notorious Freemason from Bologna. In his bitterness, he had written a great deal of abuse against the Church. In the newspaper, *Italia laica*, he had described Padre Pio as a hoaxer, a charlatan and a fraud, and accused him of taking advantage of people's naivety.

One of his nephews came down with an incurable illness. The doctors had given up all hope. One day, a friend of Del Fante, unknown to him, asked for his cure through the intercession of Padre Pio. The cure came quickly and was, humanly speaking, inexplicable.

When Del Fante heard about the intercession of Padre Pio he was utterly astonished and intensely curious. He decided to go to San Giovanni Rotondo to meet this man for himself. His interviews with Padre Pio went on for days on end. The priest put himself completely at the disposal of the Freemason for all that he wanted to find out about the faith. Del Fante was torn between two disturbing realities, the incontestable cure of his nephew against all human odds and the indisputable fact that, despite never having met him or known him, Padre Pio knew all about Del Fante's present life and his future! Gradually he was moved towards conversion, keeping a diary of his spiritual journey.

One by one, all his doubts faded to the point where his soul was completely enlightened. He not only became a convert but a follower of Padre Pio and testified to his powers. Later he wrote a major book on the priest entitled: *Per la Storia,* (For History), in which he gathered his own testimonies and those of others. At the time of his conversion something happened which confirmed him definitively in his faith and put a seal on it. His young wife was expecting a baby and he was very anxious because she had been unable to breast-feed her other two children. As Del Fante was on the point of leaving Padre Pio, he wanted to recommend his wife and her problem to him. He was about to speak when Padre Pio interjected with: ''Will your wife have milk for this little one?'' He was amazed because this was precisely what was on his mind at that moment. Padre Pio assured him that everything would be all right, and it was!

"Padre Pio! Give me a sign!"

Auré Caviggioli, an antique dealer from Monte Carlo, had been away from the Church for a long time. One day he went to the Rome-Termini station and, without knowing why, bought a ticket for Foggia. During the journey he dozed off and when he woke up he became aware of a strong perfume but could not identify its source.

On his arrival in Foggia, he took the bus for San Giovanni Rotondo and checked in at the hotel. Next morning, on his way to Padre Pio's Mass, he was aware of the same perfume he had smelt on the train. During the celebration he was fascinated by the priest's presence. He wanted to get near but the crowd was dense. The next day, thanks to some Brothers, he was able to get close to Padre Pio who asked him: "What do you want?" Caviggioli was embarrassed for a moment and then remembered that one of his grand-daughters, living in Switzerland, had a brain tumour, so he recommended her to his prayers. Padre Pio advised him to go home because the child had been cured. The cure, in fact, had been immediate and complete, so much so that the doctors would not take their fees as they concluded they had done nothing in this case.

This excited Caviggioli's curiosity and he went back several times to San Giovanni Rotondo to meet Padre Pio and make his confession to him. But a certain fear held him back. Two years passed and he decided to make Padre Pio a gift of a painting of the Virgin Mary carrying the child Jesus, the work of a painter of the sixteenth century. A friend who came to look at it asked Caviggioli how much it was worth. He answered that it was worth millions! But during the night Padre Pio came to him in a dream and looking at him very severely said: "What are you talking about? You only paid 25,000 liras for that painting!" When he woke up, the antique dealer recalled that, in fact, this was the price he had paid for it to a Jew who was later deported during World War II.

When Caviggioli went to San Giovanni Rotondo he presented the painting to Padre Pio who asked him: "What did you dream last night, you rogue?" and burst out laughing. The dealer told him his dream and he too laughed.

However, even on this occasion, Padre Pio would not hear his confession. Back at his hotel, alone and looking at the monastery he cried out: "Listen! Padre Pio! give me a sign that I may know when to come to confession." To his utter amazement, he had hardly finished the sentence when Padre Pio appeared before him, took him by the hand and then disappeared. Caviggioli was filled with fear and quite stunned by this. Next day the priest heard his confession and apologized for having scared him by appearing at the hotel!

A voice in the night said: "Get up and go to Padre Pio."

Luigi Rago, from Salerno, although married and a father, had the habit of looking for a good time with attractive women when he was away from home on business. One night in 1960, he was with a woman in a hotel in Foggia when he heard, interiorly, a strong, stern voice ordering him in no uncertain terms: "Get up and go find Padre Pio!"

Rago, who since his youth had given up the Church and religious practice, had no idea who Padre Pio might be but faced with this strange and imperative command he felt he had no option but to obey. He got up and dressed. To those who asked him: "Where are you going at this hour?" He replied: "I am going to see Padre Pio at San Giovanni Rotondo." At two o'clock in the morning he was at the door of the church where a crowd had gathered to attend Padre Pio's Mass. He joined them and went close to the altar where the celebration was to take place. When Padre Pio arrived, Rago felt a kind of electric shock go through his body and he followed every detail of the Mass which he saw as an enthralling show. In spite of all this he did not dare approach the friar. However from that time he felt a great desire to go to church and pray. Whenever he had occasion to be in Foggia he always went to San Giovanni Rotondo to attend Padre Pio's Mass. Back in Salerno he adopted the habit of going to a church to pray before the painting of the Madonna there. He ended up by breaking off the relationship he had with a woman who was his mistress. Yet, his soul was still far from being peaceful and serene. His sins weighed heavily on him. He went back, one day, to San Giovanni Rotondo and asked Padre Pio to hear his confession. "What's this?" Padre Pio demanded. "You have been away from the Church for many, many years, you did not pray and you gave your soul to the devil! Get out of here!" Rago was deeply ashamed but did not lose heart. Padre Pio did not forget him. He appeared to Rago in a dream, spreading his special perfume around, gave him spiritual comfort and told him of a good priest he should see. Rago went off to find him and made a general confession. From that moment he came back to the Church, was at peace with himself, and reconciled with his family and friends. He wanted to be reconciled with Padre Pio too, so he went to the priest and said: "Father the last time I was here you chased me away." Padre Pio replied: "And who can say anything against you now, my son?" This was the beginning of a spiritual friendship which had an influence on everyone who knew Rago.

A trap that worked

A trader from Genoa had to visit Foggia to negotiate an oil sale. One of his friends, who knew he had been away from the Church for a long time, planned to lay a trap for him! He asked him to make a little detour by San Giovanni Rotondo to deliver a letter to Padre Pio, hoping that his friend would meet the priest. The man accepted to do this and took the letter. At Foggia he got on the bus for San Giovanni Rotondo. Tired out by such a long journey he had but one thought in mind, to get rid of the letter as quickly as possible. When a Brother opened the door he gave him the letter and said he wanted an immediate reply because he had to be on his way. He was invited into the sacristy to wait until Padre Pio would come down and give him an answer. The trader waited a few minutes in the sacristy and began to grow impatient. Padre Pio arrived but made no impression on his visitor. The priest approached, looked him straight in the eye and asked: "Now you, what do you want?" The man answered that he just wanted a reply to the letter. "Ah yes," Padre Pio said, "the letter! But what about you? Don't you want to go to confession?" The man admitted that he had not practiced his religion for a very long time. Padre Pio asked him: "How long is it since your last confession?" "I was seven years old." said the trader. The priest looked at him in such a way that it seemed he saw into his soul, and said: "How long do you intend living this disgusting kind of life?" In a flash, the man saw how his life had been lived without God, repented, went to confession and was filled with joy! He had come to the monastery, rather unwillingly, to render a service to his friend and be done with this obligation as quickly as possible. He stayed for another week, fascinated by Padre Pio, attending his Mass and receiving communion at his hands. The trap set by the trader's friend had worked perfectly!

A spate of chain conversions

Luisa Vairo was living in London when she made a visit to San Giovanni Rotondo in September, 1925. She told the story of her own conversion and that of others linked to it.

This woman lived without giving any thought to religion. She enjoyed a life of pleasure, yet found no satisfaction in it. It was during this time of stress that she was shaken by something that happened to one of her friends. He was converted, thanks to

43

Padre Pio. The story this friend told impressed her so much that she decided to meet this famous Capuchin.

One day she arrived at San Giovanni and experienced a strange feeling within herself when she saw the poverty and destitution of the countryside and of the monastery. (With all the changes that have taken place since 1925, this is hard to imagine today!) What a contrast with the drawing-rooms of London! The woman's first reaction was that of repugnance and she wanted to escape as quickly as possible. However, she began to feel a kind of attraction to the simplicity, the serenity and tranquillity of the atmosphere. She was perplexed and terrified at the thought of meeting a priest who knew and saw everything and lived with the suffering of the stigmata. She became aware of the abyss that separated her pleasure-seeking way of life from this mysterious world and began to sob uncontrollably, disturbing those around her in the little church! Padre Pio arrived and came over to her as if he had known her all his life. "Don't be so upset, Madam! God's mercy is infinite. Jesus died on the Cross for sinners." Madame Vairo replied immediately: "I want to go to confession, Father." "Be at peace, Madam," the priest answered. "Now is not the moment." "I don't even know what to say", she replied. Padre Pio advised her: "Come back this afternoon at three o'clock and I will hear your confession. Now, go and freshen up, then come and find me. If you don't know what to say I will do the talking for you!"

The woman did exactly as she was told but her mind was agitated and in a state of utter confusion, to the extent that she could not prepare properly for her confession. When she came back to Padre Pio he took the initiative and enumerated all the sins she had ever committed, giving the place, the time and the circumstances of each one until she went pale as she listened. Padre Pio omitted one sin and asked her: "Is there anything else you can recall?" The penitent was fully aware of this particular sin she had committed. She wondered about it. Should she admit to it or not? Finally, she decided she would acknowledge it. Padre Pio, radiant, cried out: That's what I was waiting for!" He then absolved her from all her sins.

Madame Vairo, now forgiven, felt like a new person. Not only did she want to spend some more time with the priest who had given her new life but she imposed a severe penance on herself to expiate her sins. One day she decided to walk barefoot to the monastery in freezing rain and sleet. She arrived soaked through and with bleeding feet. When Padre Pio saw her in this state, he told her that this was a rather heavy penance to undertake, then he added: "But this water is not really wet!" Madame Vairo's clothes were dried on the spot!

And that is not the end. Madame Vairo had a son who, as she had been, was away from the Church. In the fervour of her newfound life she wrote to him telling the wonderful story of her conversion and her enthusiasm over Padre Pio. She invited him to join her at San Giovanni Rotondo. Her son wanted nothing to do with all this and replied that he would never come, not even out of curiosity. Padre Pio urged the mother to persevere in prayer for her son, assuring her that he too would one day be converted. Some time later, a French friend brought her a newspaper which carried the story that the ship her son was on had been sunk and many passengers had been drowned. She was convinced that her son was among them and was plunged into a state of deep distress and hopelessness. When Padre Pio learned the reason for her anguish, he asked: "Who told you that your son was dead and reduced you to this state?" She replied: "Who can tell me if he is alive?" The priest recollected himself in prayer and declared: "Thanks be to God! Your son is alive and he can be found in such and such a place." He pinpointed the place with precision. The mother wrote immediately to the address at the same time as the survivor was writing to reassure her of his safety. The letters crossed and the son was mystified as to how his mother could have known where he was staying. This intrigued him so much that he went to San Giovanni Rotondo to clear up the mystery.

When he arrived his mother asked him to fast in preparation for confession and to receive Holy Communion from Padre Pio. The young man agreed to do this then excused himself to go to the market-place promising to be back shortly. While he was out he bought two eggs which he guzzled followed by a bunch of grapes. He then returned to his mother in the sacristy. When Padre Pio arrived Madame Vairo introduced her son saying: "Father, this is the child I spoke to you about." Padre Pio looked at him somewhat ironically, saying: "What a fraud! What a little liar!" and turning to his mother said: "You believe, don't you, my poor woman, that he has been fasting?" The young man wanted to intervene and ask the priest: "Why are you treating me in this way? You don't even know me!" But Padre Pio broke in saying: "Do you still want to insist that you were fasting? What about the eggs and the bunch of grapes you have eaten?" The young man gave in saying: "Father, forgive me. I believe!" He, in his turn, became a convert.

Called in his sleep

A young engineer from Bologna, who had been away from the Church for years, dreamt one night of Padre Pio. The friar gazed at him for a long time and then disappeared after saying: "It is fortunate for you that you could sustain my scrutiny!" The young man had no idea who Padre Pio was and had never even heard of him. The dream intrigued him very much so he decided to make some inquiries. One day, he heard someone mention the priest. His feelings were very mixed. He had a great desire to meet this man and at the same time he felt his conscience pricking him. He wanted to come out of this situation but did not feel he had the inner strength to do so. So he sank back into his lethargy and eight years went by.

It took a catastrophe to wake him out of his apathy. An earthquake shook Bologna. The engineer decided to visit Padre Pio and took the train to San Giovanni Rotondo. After several kilometers he felt ill and had to go back home. To explain this inconvenience he wrote to Padre Pio. The priest replied through a confrère, counselling him to be patient, to pray and engage in charitable work until the right moment came along. Some time later after gathering information from some followers of Padre Pio, he went off to San Giovanni Rotondo. When he saw Padre Pio at the monastery he recognized him; he looked exactly as he had in the dream eight years earlier. He fell on his knees, weeping and managed to blurt out: "I have known of your reputation for holiness for eight years!" Padre Pio replied: "What good has it done you? You have lived as you wished! Change your life, my son!" This time, the engineer readily accepted Padre Pio's advice. He went to confession and received absolution. Utterly changed, he returned to Bologna and told the whole story to his family and friends.

The return of the lost artist

Professor Felice Checcacci from Genoa was a writer and composer of some renown and a proverbial "lost sheep"! For about forty years he had lived in Asia, had given up his Christian identity and had embraced other cults to the point that he believed Christianity to be an offshoot of Brahmanism and Buddhism.

On his return to Italy he had occasion to read the work of Alberto Del Fante on Padre Pio: *Dal dubbio alla fede* (*From doubt to Faith*) and this other book by the same author *Per la Storia* (*For History*). These books disturbed him deeply. One night he dreamt that Padre Pio said to him: "Come and see me!" He did not pay any heed to it. Two or three months later the priest appeared to him in another dream saying: "I waited for you but you did not come!" Still, he was unaffected.

Some time later, when he was lying awake, the professor saw Padre Pio come into his room and approach the bed saying: "If you can't come to see me, at least write!" Checcacci was left in no doubt about the presence of Padre Pio. He saw him, heard him speak and was terrified! He got out of bed to speak to the priest but he had already disappeared.

Next morning he wrote to Padre Pio asking him for peace of soul. Two days later, in the afternoon, he felt his body shake from head to toe and at the same time heard an interior voice say to him: "Faith is not up for discussion. You either accept it blindly or you reject it. There is no in-between. You must make the choice." Suddenly a great light filled his soul, he found his faith again, and bore witness to this by living in great peace of mind.

The fasting labourer

At San Martino in Pensilis lived a labourer called Andrea Bacile. This man never went to the Church, never received the Sacraments and saw himself as an atheist without any use for religion. He was married and had children, loved his wife and family very much and looked after them well. However, he did not always agree with his wife. One night they had a violent row and he went to bed in a foul mood. He was about to put out the bedroom light when, suddenly, he saw Padre Pio standing in front of him. It was not difficult to identify him from the many photographs and drawings he had seen of this priest. Without hesitation Bacile asked if he could go to confession. Padre Pio replied: "No!" and disappeared.

Next day Bacile made up with his wife and, fasting, set out on the road to San Giovanni Rotondo.

It took him three days to reach the monastery where he arrived exhausted and very hungry but he wanted to go immediately to confession. After giving him absolution Padre Pio said, without knowing anything about this man, "Now go and eat!"

Justified harshness

A woman from England travelled to San Giovanni Rotondo to go to Padre Pio for confession but when he saw her behind the screen he violently closed the grill, saying to her: "I have no time for someone like you!" It is not difficult to imagine how stunned this woman was as well as those who witnessed what had happened. Why did Padre Pio treat this penitent so badly? Some of those close to the priest felt it was their duty to tell him that this woman had come a long distance to have his absolution. But their plea fell on deaf ears! This went on for twenty days. The Englishwoman went each day to the confessional and each day she was sent away. Finally Padre Pio decided to hear her confession. When she complained to him about having to wait so long he said: "How can you be so blind? Instead of moaning about my severity, ask yourself how the mercy of God could possibly come to you after so many years of sacrilege. Do you realize what a terrible thing you have done? Whoever commits a sacrilege is condemned out of hand and cannot be saved without a special grace which can only come through someone close to God. Although you were in mortal sin, you went to Holy Communion with your mother and husband, year after year, just to keep up appearances." Padre Pio's instant revelation of this woman's past profoundly affected her. She repented of her past, went to confession and, at last, got absolution. Her life was completely changed and she lived her Christian commitment fully to make up for her past sins.

A murder was planned... but...

The man who, one day, came to Padre Pio, was of that type of hard, cold criminals who will stop at nothing. This individual wanted to get rid of his wife but in such a way that his crime would be cloaked with a motive of piety.

Under the pretext of going to see Padre Pio he brought his wife with him to San Giovanni Rotondo where he planned to kill her in a most diabolical way. On arriving at the monastery he went through the Capuchins' church to the sacristy. Padre Pio was there, talking to some people. When he saw the man, he left them abruptly, went to the man and began to push him violently towards the door, shouting at the top of his voice: "Get out! Get out! Don't you know it is forbidden to stain your hands with blood? Get out!"

The unfortunate man was dumbfounded and, livid with rage, bolted out of the church, to the astonishment of everyone there. However, the strong words and behaviour of Padre Pio made such an impression on him that he could not get a wink of sleep all night. He began to understand the horror of what he was planning and, touched by grace, was a different man in the morning.

He went to the monastery and this time Padre Pio received him with great tenderness, heard his confession and gave him absolution. To crown everything Padre Pio asked him before he left: "You have always wanted children haven't you?" (Blast! How could the priest have known that? He had never mentioned this to anyone!) The priest went on: "Do not offend God anymore and you will have a son." A year later the man returned to Padre Pio to celebrate his son's baptism and the confirmation of his conversion.

4

A PENETRATING GAZE

Many who came to Padre Pio were quite taken aback and astounded by the revelations he made to them about their lives, past and present. Sometimes, he even revealed to them events that would happen in the future, and these always took place! It could be said that Padre Pio read the destiny of individuals like an open book.

How can these things be explained? As far as I am concerned, I think that, in these cases, Padre Pio was able to reach into the individual lives of those who came to him because he could see them surrounded with God's powerful Light. This helped him to adapt his treatment of souls in the way he thought best, according to his conscience. Moreover, he told one of his confrères that he dealt with souls in the way the Lord showed him. In the following pages I offer some stories of this kind. Others have already been told about the conversion of some of the people mentioned.

Like a page in a diary

A priest set out on a long journey to visit Padre Pio and make his confession to him. He had to change trains at Bologna and wait a very long time for his connection. By this time he was rather tired and went to a hotel room where he fell fast asleep and only woke up at three in the afternoon! He had not been able to say his Mass, because at that time Mass had to be celebrated in the morning. It was an unintentional mistake to which he did not attach a great deal of importance. But Padre Pio did not see it this way! When the priest arrived, Padre Pio asked him, after his confession and absolution: "My brother! Have you perhaps forgotten something?" The priest replied: "No, Father." Padre Pio suggested that he take time to search his soul which he did thoroughly and still came up with nothing. Then Padre Pio said to him: "My son, you arrived at Bologna railway station yesterday morning. The churches were closed but instead of waiting until they opened you went to a hotel and fell asleep until three in the afternoon and therefore you were too late to celebrate Mass. I know you did not do this on purpose but it was an act of negligence which hurt Our Lord." By giving this priest a resumé, like a page from a diary, of all that had happened the preceding day, Padre Pio wanted to drive home to him the importance of the Mass in the life of a man consecrated to the priesthood.

"Call him Pio! Call him Francis!"

An officer in the carabinieri had no time for Padre Pio. He did not think highly of him and took every opportunity to put him down. One day, however, he decided to meet him in person and went to San Giovanni Rotondo. When Padre Pio saw him he asked point-blank: "Why do you tell all these cock and bull stories about me when you have never even met me? Look and see first, judge for yourself and then say what you want!" The officer was won over, as he began to understand and appreciate Padre Pio. Some time later he said to the priest: "Father my wife is expecting a baby! What should we call it?" Padre Pio replied immediately: "Call him Pio." "And what if it's a girl?" Padre Pio repeated, very clearly: "I told you to call him Pio!" A boy was born and they named him Pio.

Two years later this father came back to see Padre Pio and to tell him his wife was pregnant again. "So what name should we give this time?" he asked. Padre Pio answered: "Call him Francis." The officer raised some doubts: "Father, we had a boy last time but this sort of thing does not necessarily come in series!" Padre Pio cried out: "Man of little faith!" The officer's wife gave birth to a boy and they called him Francis.

"He's crazy!"

A doctor friend of mine went to Padre Pio one day, just at the same time as the famous actor, Carlo

Campanini and a veterinarian from Bologna. Padre Pio told Campanini to put his son in a home. When the veterinarian showed him an X-Ray of his son who was suspected of having brain tumour the priest told him not to worry but to take his son back to Bologna assuring him that there was nothing wrong.

All this came true. At the time however, the doctor thought it all a bit risky. "He's crazy!" he said to himself. He was even more convinced of this when Padre Pio came up to him and putting his hand on his head said: "You are a bit absent-minded aren't you?" The doctor said to himself: "Now I know for sure that he is completely crazy!" He had, in fact, an excellent memory, so good that he could remember all the names of the many types of medicine and some had very strange names indeed! This is why he knew it was out of the question that he could be forgetful. After his visit to Padre Pio, he remembered that before going to see him he had gone into a local bar for a coffee. As he had no small change he had handed the waiter a ten-thousand-lira bill. The waiter had put the change down on the counter but the doctor had forgotten to pick it up. When he recalled this he went back to the place but the barman pretended he knew nothing about it. He said he had given him the change and that was that! My friend tried to explain as well as he could that he had not taken the change, but there was nothing to be done. In the end he said to himself: "It's not Padre Pio's who's crazy but I am, since I ended up paying ten thousand liras for a thirty-lira cup of coffee!"

A fifty-year-long misunderstanding

One of the first photographers of Padre Pio's stigmata, in their first stages, was a man called Modesto Vinelli. He made copies of his photographs and sold them everywhere to make Padre Pio known. One day he arrived at Rodi Garganico and met a man who wanted to know nothing about Padre Pio. A rather heated discussion followed which led to violence. Vinelli defended the priest against the insults, curses and blasphemies of the other man. After a while Vinelli gave way to his anger and began punching and kicking the man. The man was injured and Vinelli arrested and put in jail for forty days.

When he came out he went to Padre Pio and said to him: "Father, I was sent to prison because of you!" Padre Pio asked: "Because of me? What did you do?" Vinelli told him all that had happened at Rodi Garganico. The priest advised Vinelli to be patient with those who did not think along the same lines, and especially that he, Vinelli, had to keep his fists to himself, adding: "Modesto, remember we still have fifty years ahead of us!" What did Padre Pio mean by these words? Probably the following: "We must be patient with those who do not think as we do because, with time, the truth will come out and we have fifty years ahead of us for that." Unfortunately Vinelli did not understand his words in this way. He thought he, personally, had only fifty years to live!

Every year, on September 20th, Vinelli went to the monastery for the anniversary of Padre Pio's stigmata and as the years went by he heard the priest tell him how many years remained. On the twenty-fifth year, as usual on this date, Vinelli went to see Padre Pio who said to him: "Modesto, twenty-five years have passed!" The photographer found some consolation in the fact that if twenty-five years had gone it was equally true that twenty-five years remained. However he began to get worried and his anxiety only increased with the passing years. On September 20th, 1968, two days before Padre Pio's death, Vinelli went to see him. This time the priest said to him: "Modesto, the fifty years are over!" Vinelli was very upset by this, and near to breaking point, because he thought Padre Pio was telling him *he* would die. The shock was so intense that he nearly collapsed. Someone explained to him that the priest was speaking of his own death which he foresaw as imminent and not that of Modesto. In fact, on the night of September 22nd-23rd 1968, Padre Pio died. In spite of feeling sad at losing such a dear friend, Vinelli was relieved when the misunderstanding was cleared up! He lived another fifteen years and died on March 2nd, 1983.

"No! You will forget it!"

Among the many, many peole who came to see Padre Pio was Archbishop Marcel Lefebvre who, later clinging stubbornly to Catholic Tradition, as he called it, questioned the authority of Vatican II and was removed from office by Pope Paul VI.

The archbishop had a meeting with Padre Pio in the presence of Professor Bruno Rabajotti. This witness reported that at a particular moment Padre Pio looked at Lefebvre very sternly and said: "Never cause discord among your brothers and always practice the rule of obedience, above all when it seems to you that the errors of those in authority are all the more serious. There is no other road than that of obedience, especially for those of us who have made this vow."

Padre Pio could give this advice because he had had to obey some rather questionable orders himself. His attitude was to put this in God's hands because He would find a way for truth to triumph. It seems that Archbishop Lefebvre did not see things in quite the same way even if he did respond to Padre Pio with: "I will remember that, Father." Padre Pio looked at him intensely and, seeing what would soon happen, said: No! You will forget it! You will tear apart the community of the faithful, oppose the will of your superiors and even go against the orders of the pope himself and this will happen quite soon. You will forget the promise you made here today, and the whole Church will be hurt by you. Don't set yourself up as a judge. Don't take powers that do not belong to you and do not consider yourself as the voice of God's People, as God already speaks to them. Do not sow discord and dissension. However, I know this is what you will do!"

Unfortunately, the truth of Padre Pio's prophecy is obvious to everyone.

Don't play games with suffering

Professor Bruno Rabajotti tells how, one day, a group made up of two laymen, a religious from the monastery at San Giovanni and a priest decided to play a rather bad joke on Padre Pio. They persuaded a man of about thirty-five to pretend he was paralyzed.

They went together to the monastery and waited in the parlour for Padre Pio on the pretence that they had brought someone for a cure. It was a Friday, the day on which Padre Pio's sufferings were particularly intense. At times, he was in such agony that he could not come down to the church for Mass or Confessions. He was called to the parlour and arrived there with great difficulty. When he reached the doorway he immediately looked at the false paralytic and came towards him saying: "You are here pretending to be ill but your real illness is in your soul. It has wounds you cannot begin to imagine! Understand this, you cannot play games with suffering. God does not will it. The illness you feigned today will strike your family. You brought on this misfortune. You wanted suffering!" Having said this, Padre Pio looked at him for a few moments and then went away.

The young man was very shaken by these words and went home as quickly as he could. When he got there he learned that his brother had been knocked down by a car. He had been taken immediately to the hospital where he was given emergency treatment but the doctors could do nothing to save his legs. He would be paralyzed for life.

The following Sunday there was a conference at the monastery and Padre Pio was present. When it ended, the priest got up to leave when he saw the false paralytic in the crowd. The young man threw himself at Padre Pio's feet crying: "Have mercy on me, Father, for I have sinned. My brother was not the one who sinned. Cure him and let God do to me what He wants!" Padre Pio replied: "It is not for me to grant you pardon but go ask it of the priest who went along with your charade. And may you be as worthy of what you ask as you deserved what happened to you."

The following week, as he was passing a line of people waiting for confession, Padre Pio noticed the same man curled up in a corner, praying. Generally he did not stop but he hesitated for a moment, puzzled. He went towards the unfortunate man, laid his hands on him and whispered something in his ear.

Later, it was revealed that the false paralytic's brother had been cured in an extraordinary way and the unfortunate joker became one of Padre Pio's most fervent spiritual sons.

The pictures did not cause the blasphemy

In 1926, a bus driver from San Severo took pilgrims to the grotto at Monte Sant'Angelo. This had become a shrine to St. Michael the Archangel who had appeared there and had been venerated for centuries.

The driver, a follower of Padre Pio, attended Mass with the pilgrims then went off for a walk around the town. He came to a bakery where they were making cracker biscuits, a specialty of the area, and he went in to order some to share with the pilgrims. When he received the bag, he realized that only half the amount had been given to him. This irritated him so much that he let slip a blasphemy! He went back to the pilgrims and drove them to San Giovanni Rotondo where they went to Padre Pio for confession. When he had finished, the priest turned to the driver and said: "And you my son? Don't you want even a blessing?" He replied that he really had nothing to confess and that his conscience was at peace. Padre Pio insisted so he went into the confessional. The priest asked him what he had been doing all day. The driver told him he had been to Mass with the pilgrims at Sant'Angelo and that he had bought some pictures. The priest said to him: "But it was not the pictures that made you blaspheme but something you ate!" The man remembered the blasphemy he had uttered on leaving the bakery. Padre Pio went on: "You also insulted the cart driver who did not keep to his right!" All this was true.

Words were unnecessary

The next two incidents happened to me so I am a prime witness. For a long time I had been worried about a spiritual problem I could not put right because I did not know its causes. I had never spoken to anyone about this. One day I got the opportunity I needed to talk about it.

A friend who lived at San Giovanni Rotondo, well known to the Capuchins there, invited me to stay in his home and arranged for me to meet Padre Pio. I was greeted by Father Venanzo one of the priests who scheduled visits to Padre Pio. He was told in advance to expect me and brought me in saying: "Wait here. Padre Pio will not be long, but this is

Friday and the wounds bleed more profusely. He has gone to the kitchen to wash." While waiting, I went over in my mind all that I wanted to say to present my situation in the most precise and clear way possible.

Shortly afterwards, I saw Padre Pio coming down the corridor. As he approached me, and without giving me time to speak, he whispered in my ear: "This is the reason for your situation!" and he summed it up in a single sentence. Although thirty years have gone by since he said this, I remember it word for word as if it were yesterday! I was completely thrown by this. There was no need to talk because the priest had gone right to the heart of the problem and found its cause. After this Padre Pio walked away, then came back and repeated what he had said so that there would be no doubt in my mind. He started on his way up to his cell and, half-way there, he turned round and said: "Where are you saying Mass tomorrow?" Still a bit shaken by all that had happened I answered vaguely: "I don't know Father." "You don't want to come here to say it?" I replied: "Yes, yes Father! I will say Mass here!" He finished by saying: "Yes, come! You must say Mass here tomorrow." He went on up the stairs and disappeared along the corridor.

When I returned to my friend's house, seeing I was deep in thought, everyone questioned me saying: "What's the matter with you, Father Cataneo?" I told them Padre Pio had read my soul and solved my problem. When they heard this they exclaimed: "So, what people say about him is true. You know, here in San Giovanni, we hear so many things, but if *you* tell us that this is what happened then it is true!" I said to them: "You can be sure that it is really true. I am an irrefutable proof of that."

"This spiritual life"

At one time, priests who were not resident in San Giovanni Rotondo could line up to go to Padre Pio for confession, one after every five lay penitents. I wanted to speak to him on certain matters but realized it was now much more difficult to have a private talk with him than when I had first met him. So many people wanted to get near him that the crowds had to be organized and directed.

I thought the best thing to do, if I wanted to go to Confession to him, was to make use of the arrangement offered to non-resident priests and speak my heart to him in the confessional. I was aware that many people who wanted to go to Confession were, perhaps, in greater need than I so I decided to make a thorough preparation so that I would not waste time with the priest.

I made my examination of conscience in the bus from Foggia on my way to San Giovanni Rotondo. I recall that, on a bend in the road where the town came into view, I finished my examination, thinking to myself: "This spiritual life... What an adventure! It's like walking on glass!" Then my mind turned to other things. The bus dropped me off at the Capuchin monastery. I went to the chapel and waited in line where Padre Pio was hearing confessions. When my turn came I opened my heart to him. Padre Pio gave me the answers I was waiting for and I received his absolution. Just as I was about to get up off my knees he turned to me, with a twinkle in his eye, and said: "This spiritual life... What an adventure! It's like walking on glass, isn't it?" He had read my thoughts even before I reached San Giovanni Rotondo and he repeated them word for word although I had already forgotten them! I was astonished but at the same time received great encouragement from this reflection of his because it pointed to the difficulties we meet in all spiritual life and the temptation to give up. In repeating what I had thought, Padre Pio was certainly saying to me: "You think you have difficulties? What should I say about mine? Courage!"

A petty thief is caught

Among the people who flocked to Padre Pio there were always some who wanted to snatch some relic from him out of devotion or fanatic zeal. He could not stand this as it surrounded him with the kind of aura of sanctity which he detested. He reacted every time it happened, and sometimes harshly: such was his character. Someone pointed out to him that this response could upset people but Padre Pio showed him his torn habit and slashed Franciscan cord saying: "And if I don't react, where will it all end?"

One evening, after Office he went down to the garden with some friends and doctors from the *Casa Sollievo della Sofferenza*, a hospital he had founded. Cosimo Iadanza, a fellow-countryman of Padre Pio was in the group. The priest had forgotten his handkerchief. He called Cosimo and said: "Here

Cosimo, would you take the key to my cell and fetch me a handkerchief. I need one!" Cosimo took the key and went to the friar's cell. He found a handkerchief but could not resist the temptation to take something else to keep as a relic. He went back to the garden, looking innocent of the whole affair, and gave Padre Pio the handkerchief. The priest gave him a strange look and said: "Go back this minute to my room and replace what you have put in your pocket." Cosimo blushed. He really believed he could get off with taking the relic because no one had seen him. He had not reckoned with Padre Pio's penetrating mind!

He smelt a rat!

One of Padre Pio's American benefactors came to San Giovanni Rotondo to see the priest. They had hardly met when Padre Pio pushed him aside brusquely saying: "Go away! I do not know you!" The poor man was upset and wondered why he was being treated in this way.

He went off to find Father Alberto D'Apolito, who lived at San Severo, thinking that if the priest would come with him to Padre Pio he might recognize him and receive him. Father D'Apolito thought that if Padre Pio had treated the American that badly there was something not quite right. He smelt a rat! (In fact, the American had a mistress!) However, Father D'Apolito accompanied his visitor to San Giovanni Rotondo but he warned the man: "You'll see! The minute he sees us he will chase both of us away!" Sure enough, as soon as Padre Pio saw him accompanied by Father D'apolito he shouted: "So you needed someone to plead for you! Go away, both of you!"

So they left. When Father Alberto heard that the American was going to Assisi and Padua he advised him to go to confession at one of these shrines. He did as the priest had said. Before leaving for America the traveller wanted to go back to San Giovanni Rotondo to meet Padre Pio. Again, Father Alberto went with him. This time, Padre Pio received him with great kindness, thanked him for his generosity, made a few requests, embraced and blessed him saying: "When you return to America, make sure you are a good Christian. You understand?" The man promised but later on, because of weakness, fell back into his old ways.

The following year he wanted to go back to San Giovanni Rotondo and asked Padre Pio, through Father Alberto, if he might return. Padre Pio replied: "No!"

Time went by and eventually the benefactor ended the relationship with his mistress to be with his wife and family. Again, he asked Padre Pio if he could come and see him. This time the priest said: "Yes!" He arrived just in time to receive Padre Pio's blessing because he died very soon afterwards.

Answering a sealed letter

A parish priest who saw so many of his people go to Padre Pio was resentful of this and wanted to trap Padre Pio by sending him a letter. In it he asked the friar a question. He sealed the letter and gave it to one of his parishioners who was going to San Giovanni Rotondo, insisting that he give the letter into the hands of Padre Pio, personally, and wait for a reply. The man agreed to do this and set out for San Giovanni Rotondo with a parish group. When he arrived Padre Pio welcomed the man with all the others then singled him out and approached him saying: "Take out the letter you have in your pocket and write down this reply on the envelope." The messenger brought out the letter and, with his big handwriting, wrote down the reply dictated by the friar.

When he got home he went to the parish priest and told him that Padre Pio had replied to his letter without even opening it! The priest read the reply the parishioner had written on the sealed envelope and to his astonishment saw that this was the exact answer to the question he had asked Padre Pio!

As you can see, it was not easy to ensnare Padre Pio!

"Padre Pio sent us."

It is well known that Pope Benedict XV held Padre Pio in high esteem. In his entourage, however, some considered the priest to be an imposter. Among them was a bishop who believed it was his duty to warn the pope against Padre Pio. Benedict XV pointed out to him that before taking sides against the friar he should meet him and get to know all about him. He advised him to go to San Giovanni Rotondo and see things for himself and discover the truth about Padre Pio.

When he arrived at Foggia he saw two Capuchins coming towards him to greet him. They explained that Padre Pio had sent them to accompany him to San Giovanni. Astonished, the bishop told them that no one knew of his visit to San Giovanni, least of all, Padre Pio! The two Capuchins told him that Padre Pio had given them the description of a bishop, sent by the pope, telling them to accompany him to San Giovanni. The bishop was very embarrassed by all this. What should he do? Should he go or not? He realized that if the priest already knew of his coming he was likely to know, also, what he had said against him to the Pope. To save face, he decided to make up the excuse of having a rather urgent appointment to keep, and returned to Rome.

"Coward!"

It was a well known fact that Padre Pio was not intimidated by anything or anyone. He was very forthright and frank in what he had to say and even, at times, harsh, when his conscience called for it. I think this behaviour sprang from the fact that being so deeply rooted in God he could deal with people in great freedom.

No one could apply to him what Jesus said to his disciples one day: "If someone disowns me before men, the Son of Man will disown him before the Father." He wanted his spiritual sons to behave like him. The following incident should be understood in this context.

One of his spiritual sons in Rome had the habit of raising his hat when passing a church to honour the presence of the Blessed Sacrament there. One day he was out with friends who were more interested in the trifles and things of the world. They passed by a church and he was ashamed to raise his hat in their company. At that moment he heard a loud cry in his ear: "Coward!" Later when he returned to San Giovanni Rotondo and met Padre Pio, the priest said to him: "Watch out! This time you just got a reprimand but next time you'll get your ears boxed!"

"You will die in eight days!"

To tell a young policeman in full vigour that he would die in eight days was not a pleasant task but, because of his gift of foresight Padre Pio felt compelled to do so. He tried to be as tactful and gentle as he could.

One day when he was putting away vestments in the sacristy after Mass, Padre Pio turned to one of the two policemen posted at the door to protect him from the crowds. "When I have finished my thanksgiving prayers," he said, "follow me to my cell. I want to speak with you." The young policeman was delighted but when he was alone with the priest his delight turned to sadness. Padre Pio said to him: "Listen my son, in about eight days you will be going to your father's house and there you will die."

The young man did not want to believe this and told Padre Pio he was in perfect health. But the priest would not be put off and added: "Don't worry! You will feel even better in eight days. What is life anyway but a pilgrimage. We are on a journey, my son." He advised him to ask for some time off to arrange his affairs. The young man asked if he could tell anyone about what had transpired between them. Padre Pio replied: "No! Not at the moment. Wait till you get home."

It was not easy for the young officer to get permission to go home because his Chief could not see the necessity for this and the young man could not tell him of Padre Pio's prophecy. The priest had to intervene so that the officer could get the permission he needed. At home he told his astonished and unbelieving family what Padre Pio had said. He put his affairs in order and eight days later he died suddenly.

She did not believe Padre Pio but...

Father Constantino Capobianco tells the story that one day, on the train to Rome, he sat down beside a woman travelling with her brother who worked in Public Security. Both were from Pietrelcina. The woman, dressed in black, seemed very upset. After talking with them for a while the priest learned that they were returning home from San Giovanni Rotondo where they had spoken to Padre Pio and told them of their anxiety about the woman's husband. He was a sailor, and they were afraid he had gone down with his cruiser. Padre Pio had told them not to worry and to trust in the Lord. He had told the grieving woman: "In a few days you will get some good news!" She was so convinced that her husband was dead that she did not believe Padre Pio.

A few days after her return to Pietrelcina she received a telegram from her husband! He told her not to worry as he was safe. The submarine that had torpedoed the cruiser had picked up the survivors and he was among them, safe in England. His wife now knew that Padre Pio's words were to be trusted!

Marocchino's goldfinch

At the time when Padre Pio was spiritual director of the monastery at San Giovanni there was, among the postulants, a young man nicknamed *Marocchino*. This novice loved the arts and nature.

One day a goldfinch flew in from the garden and got trapped in the corridor running alongside the friars' refectory. When Marocchino saw it he wanted to catch and keep it in a cage for his enjoyment. He went after it but the bird flew and hopped around from place to place, zigzagging as it went. Eventually it got itself stuck in a corner near the kitchen. *Marocchino* ran forward to catch it but at that very moment the bell for prayer rang so he had to give up the chase and go to chapel.

Instead of praying, however, he worked out plans to catch the bird, make the cage and choose the best place to put it. During supper he kept on thinking about the bird. On leaving the refectory he had only one thought in his head, to catch the bird! Padre Pio who had been reading his thoughts during prayer and in the refectory called the young man over: "You are losing your senses over this bird!" He went over the ideas, one by one, that had come to the postulant at prayer and during supper.

Later, *Marocchino* became known as Father Vittore and revealed all this to Father Capobianco: "When I heard Padre Pio reveal all my thoughts, one by one, with precision, accuracy and clarity, leaving nothing uncovered, I was bewildered and stood there with my head bowed like someone protecting himself from a raging storm overhead!"

Answer to a forgotten question

When news got out that Padre Pio had received the stigmata, crowds came running to the monastery at San Giovanni Rotondo. Among the first to come were some French priests led by Abbé Benoît, Secretary General of the Institut Catholique in Lille.

He had a problem with which he had been struggling for years without finding a solution but, with the passage of time, he had forgotten about it. At San Giovanni Rotondo he and the other priests were received by Padre Pio. He did not experience anything special on seeing him for the first time. As they were about to leave, the priests asked Padre Pio to autograph some pictures. He willingly did as they asked. When he came to Abbé Benoît however, instead of writing on the picture he held out, he took the breviary from under the Abbé's arm, flicked through to find a blank page and wrote down a sentence. When Abbé Benoît read it he realized that this was the answer to his long forgotten problem.

He understood then that Padre Pio was not the simple priest he had taken him for but one of those who, gifted by God, read the past of others.

"You are on your last legs!"

Father Teofilo Dal Pozzo, Provincial Superior at this particular time, was preaching at the church of San Eligio in Foggia and, over and above, took on the task of replacing one of the friars at San Giovanni Rotondo, who was away preaching for the Month of Mary. He had to drive back and forth in a small car between Foggia and San Giovanni Rotondo.

Through an interior revelation Padre Pio knew that the Provincial did not have long to live and he was anxious about the amount of work he had taken on. At the beginning Padre Pio did not say anything but later he felt it his duty to warn him. He called Father Teofilo and said to him: "What on earth are you doing? Do you realize that you are on your last legs?"

The priest did not pay much attention to Padre Pio's words believing him to be joking. He was, after all, in good health and in full activity. Three or four months later an investigation of stomach pains revealed he had a tumour. Within a month he was dead.

A delayed departure

Father Paolino di Casacalenda, who was Superior of the monastery when Padre Pio received the stigmata and later became Provincial Superior, had a sister living in San Giovanni. He went there often either to visit Padre Pio or to see his sister. On the particular day this incident happened, he was in a great hurry!

After having eaten with his confrères he noticed Padre Pio leaving without bidding him goodbye. He called over to him: "So, Padre Pio, you are going away without embracing me!" Padre Pio replied: "Reverend Father, you will not be leaving today." Father Paolino assured him that he was most certainly leaving and that the car and driver were waiting for him at his sister's door! Padre Pio simply repeated that he would not be leaving that day. He added that if the Provincial wanted to be embraced even twice that was all right with him, but he would not be leaving that day!

Father Paolino was convinced that Padre Pio was making fun of him so he took his leave of everyone and went to his sister's house. When he got there he found the driver working on the car engine. He told the priest it was a minor problem and would not prevent his departure. However, after time and effort it became obvious the trouble was more serious than the driver thought. It was a job for a mechanic which meant they could not leave until the next day.

The Provincial went back to the monastery to spend the night and when Padre Pio saw him he said: "Well Father! What did I tell you?"

"In fifteen days you will die!"

There was a priest in Mantova who had led an exemplary life, full of virtue. One night Padre Pio appeared to him in a dream and after congratulating him on his good life announced that it would soon come to an end. He told the priest he would die in fifteen days and that he should use the time well to prepare for a perfect ending to this final stage of his earthly journey.

The next morning the priest told those around him about the dream and what Padre Pio had said to him about his approaching death. They did not attach much importance to all this. After all, it was only a dream! The priest thought otherwise and prepared for death with great care. One morning, fifteen days later, he was found dead in his bedroom.

5

WORLDWIDE "TRAVELS"

Padre Pio had the gift of bilocation, that is, he could be present and active in two places at the same time. Although he had never been away from the monastery at San Giovanni Rotondo from 1916 until his death in 1968, his presence was noticed in different parts of the world, either in person or by a lingering perfume associated with him.

One day, in conversation with some of his confrères on this subject he said: "The one to whom this happens knows what he wants, where he is going and why, but he does not know whether it is only his spirit that moves or whether he is present there body and soul." This remains a mystery of the Power of God. Here are a few episodes relating to this phenomenon.

Deathbed absolution in Turin

One day Padre Pio paused in front of a window in the corridor of the monastery at San Giovanni

Rotondo. Suddenly he was caught up by some distant vision and rooted to the spot. A friar passing that way went up to him, greeted him and kissed his hand but Padre Pio was oblivious to all this. He was completely absorbed in his thoughts and pronouncing the words of absolution used in the confessional. When he came round again he noticed some of the friars had gathered around him: "Ah! You are here! I did not notice. I was contemplating the mountain."

A few days later, the Superior of San Giovanni Rotondo received a telegram thanking him for having sent Padre Pio to Turin to give absolution to a sick man just at the moment of his death.

"Go ahead! I will follow you."

In September 1955, some people from the parish of Our Lady of Grace of San Severo, went on a group pilgrimage, accompanied by some Capuchins, to the shrine of Our Lady of Tears in Syracuse. The priests came to Padre Pio before setting out on their journey, to ask his prayers and blessing but also to invite him to join them if he so wished. At this invitation Padre Pio said: "Go ahead! I will follow you." However, he did not leave San Giovanni Rotondo.

The pilgrims started out and when they came within the vicinity of Cosenza they saw a huge field of melons. They could not resist the urge to feast on them. They stopped the bus, bought some from the farmer, and gorged themselves! But melons are not easy to digest, and overheated by the sun they produced quite disastrous effects! The bus set out again but could not go far as the pilgrims had to scatter around the fields to get rid of the aftermath of this meal! They finally set out and reached Syracuse without any more stops! They visited the shrine, prayed for all their intentions and took the bus home.

On the way the driver had to stop because the road was blocked. He got down to have a look and then told the travellers that he could not go through. Anxious, they all began to invoke Padre Pio to help them out of this situation. Immediately, as was normal when Padre Pio was around, there was a strong perfume which seemed to come in waves. Then the pilgrims saw some policemen on their rounds. They unblocked the road and the journey continued without incident.

On their return the priests went to find Padre Pio who had just finished saying Mass and was preparing to make his Thanksgiving. He looked at them in a good-natured way and with a slightly mocking smile said: "That was a fine show you made with those melons! And that was quite a scare on the Palermo road the other night!"

Incidents relating to the Marchioness Rizzani Boschi

The Marchioness Giovanna Rizzani Boschi told me about her experiences of Padre Pio's power of bilocation. These took place at Udine, in Rome, at San Giovanni Rotondo, in Naples and again at San Giovanni Rotondo.

Padre Pio at Udine

During a visit I made to her when she was settled in Rome, the Marchioness told me of the circumstances surrounding her birth in Udine. These same circumstances were recorded in a written account by Padre Pio himself.

He writes: "Some days ago, (this was in February 1905 when Padre Pio was a Capuchin student at the monastery in San Eloi at Panisi), a very unusual thing happened to me, a kind of adventure. One night, about eleven o'clock on the 28th of January of this year, I was in the choir with Brother Anastasio. Suddenly, I found myself far from there, in a grand house where the father was dying just as his daughter was being born. The Virgin Mary appeared to me and said: "I confide this little one to you. This is a rough diamond. Work on her, polish her and make her shine as brilliantly as possible because I will adorn myself with her." Padre Pio asked: "But how can I do this? I am just a poor clerical student and don't even know if I will ever be a priest and even if I do become a priest how can I take care of her from so far away?" The Blessed Virgin replied: "Don't worry! She will come to you but you will meet her for the first time at St. Peter's in Rome!"

This document was carefully preserved with Padre Pio's personal effects at San Giovanni Rotondo but the Marchioness Giovanna grew up without knowing of its existence and without knowing who Padre Pio was. A long time later, when she had become a faithful follower of Padre Pio and privileged to collaborate with him, she came to know about the document and asked Padre Pio about it. He confirmed the authenticity of the facts it related.

In the aisles of St. Peter's, Rome

One summer afternoon in 1922, when she was still known as Giovanna Boschi, a university student, she was walking through St. Peter's in Rome with a friend. She was looking for some knowledgeable priest to talk to so that she might clear up some doubts she had about her faith.

After looking here and there without finding anyone, she noticed a sacristan and asked if there was a priest to whom she could talk. The good man told her that it was nearly time to close the building. "Why don't you look around," he said, "and maybe you'll find a priest who has been delayed. There is still half an hour left."

Giovanna went back and forth in the area and finally noticed a young Capuchin in a confessional. She went in and told him of her doubts and was given helpful answers, then she went off to find her friend. She told her how happy she felt and asked her to wait until the Capuchin left the confessional so that she could kiss his hand. She had a good wait! The Capuchin did not come out. She went to see, but the confessional was empty. She inquired of the sacristan about where the priest might have gone but he told her he had not seen any friar. Giovanna was surprised because she knew she had seen him and spoken to him.

"Giovanna! I know you!"

The following year, she went for her very first visit to San Giovanni Rotondo, as companion to an aunt who wanted to go to Padre Pio for confession. They were shown into the corridor between the old church and the monastery. She was told the priest would pass by and she was in the front row.

When Padre Pio arrived he noticed her right away and said: "Giovanna! I know you! You were born on the day your father died." Giovanna, startled by this revelation, wondered how he knew of the circumstances of her birth. The next day she went to confession and heard Padre Pio say to her: "My daughter, at last you have come! I have waited so many years for you!" "Father," the young girl replied, "what do you want from me? I do not know you and this is the first time I have been to San Giovanni Rotondo. I came with my aunt. You must be confusing me with some other girl."

"No," Padre Pio said, "I am not confusing you with anyone else. You already know me." She insisted: "No, Father, I assure you, I do not know you." Padre Pio continued: "Last year, on a summer afternoon, you went with a friend to St. Peter's in Rome to find a priest who could throw some light on your doubts of faith. Am I right?" "Yes, Father," Giovanna replied, "you are right." He told her of the Capuchin who had listened to her, resolved her doubts and restored her peace of soul. She remembered it well. "I was that Capuchin!" Padre Pio said and then went on to tell her of the events surrounding her birth at Udine connected with the death of her father. Giovanna was deeply moved by these revelations and asked Padre Pio what she should do. He mapped out her mission in these words: "Come often to San Giovanni Rotondo and I will take care of your soul and you will learn God's Will for you." From that day on the Marchioness Boschi became Padre Pio's faithful and privileged collaborator.

A slap in the face from Padre Pio!

Although, to a certain extent, I was personally involved in this story I would not have known the sequence of events had not Marchioness Boschi told me herself. Many years ago she lived in Naples on Via del Casale near the Via Marechiaro where I lived.

I came to know her because my community had asked her husband, an engineer, to undertake some work on our house at No. 46. This meant that, on occasion, I had to call at the home of Marchioness Boschi. In the course of a conversation we spoke of Padre Pio whom I had known since 1940. From time to time she came to our community chapel for Confession and Holy Communion. One day she arrived at about nine in the morning and I went down to hear her confession and give her Communion and then went back to my room.

Later, in Rome, she asked me if, on that morning she went to confession, I had heard the sound of a slap or had looked outside the confessional — as one can read in the book by Father Alberto D'Apolito entitled: *Padre Pio da Pietrelcina.* During this conversation the marchioness said to me quite suddenly: "Do you know that the day I went to you for Confession, Padre Pio gave me a slap?" "A slap!" I said. "But I heard nothing!" "Maybe you didn't." she replied, "but I did, and how!" She then went on to explain that Padre Pio, seeing that she had developed the habit of confessing sins already mentioned in previous confessions, forbade her to do this. However, she kept on doing this until one day he said to her: "Next time you do that I will give you a slap!" On that morning he had kept his word!

Farewell to Padre Pio

During the last two weeks of September 1968, I was passing through San Giovanni Rotondo. As a rule I always went to visit Padre Pio at the monastery. When I learned that he was quite ill, I did not want to disturb him and made up my mind I would see him when he was feeling better.

On my return to Naples, several days later, I heard on the radio that Padre Pio had died. I was deeply grieved and in great sorrow and did not want to believe that he was gone. It seemed to me that Padre Pio should never die!

I wanted to know all the details about his death but the press only gave brief accounts. I was to learn all about his death later, during a visit to the Marchioness in Rome. She told me that she had to be away from San Giovanni Rotondo during the final months of Padre Pio's life. One day she heard a voice say to her: "Come immediately to San Giovanni because I am going. If you delay you will never see me again!" She set out immediately with her friend

Marguerite Hamilton and they both stayed in a small hotel near the monastery.

A few days before his death Padre Pio said to her: "This is the last Confession you will make to me. I absolve you from every sin you have committed from the age of reason until now." "Why, Father?" she asked. "I have already told you." Padre Pio replied. "I will no longer be able to hear your confession because I am going away and Jesus is coming to meet me."

Giovanna understood that Padre Pio was leaving this world. She came out of the confessional very moved and kissed his hand. She offered him 50,000 liras for the hospital, *Casa Sollievo della Sofferenza*, but Padre Pio refused it saying that soon she would need her money.

Although she assured him she had enough money for her meal and her return journey to Rome, he repeated that she would need it soon. The Marchioness went back to the hotel room she shared with her friend.

At nightfall after blessing the crowd, who had come to San Giovanni for the International Congress of Prayer Groups, Padre Pio went to his cell. This was to be his farewell to the world.

During the night of September 23rd, 1968 around 2:25 a.m., Madame Boschi suddenly woke up crying that Padre Pio was dying! Her friend, Marguerite, thought the Marchioness was having a nightmare and tried to calm her but to no avail. Quite sure of the death of Padre Pio the Marchioness wanted to rush to the monastery. Marguerite had to dress quickly and go with her. They arrived just as one of the Capuchins announced the sad news to the crowd gathered in front of the church.

A few days later she told Father Alberto D'Apolito, who doubted her assertions, that she was present when Padre Pio died. She gave him such a precise and detailed account of all that had happened that the priest was convinced she had been present, in spirit, at the dramatic last moments of this holy man. She also gave me all the details.

In General Cadorna's tent

After the disastrous defeat at Caporetto in 1917, General Luigi Cadorna fell into a deep depression and decided to commit suicide.

One night, near Treviso, before retiring to his tent, he told the guard that on no account should anyone disturb him. Then, collapsing onto a chair he took a pistol from his bedside table and loaded it. Just as he was pointing it to his head he saw a Capuchin standing before him. The priest shook his finger at him saying: "Come now, General, surely you are not going to do anything so stupid!" The officer was so overwhelmed by this happening that he forgot all about his idea of suicide. He did not know who this religious was or how he had come into his tent.

When the Capuchin had gone, the General stormed out and demanded why the guard had let the priest into his tent, contrary to his orders. The soldier, as surprised as his superior, replied that no one had gone past him. More mystified than ever, the general went back to his tent determined to get to the bottom of this incident.

Some years late, when the war was over, the press began to write about a certain Padre Pio, a religious with the stigmata and miraculous powers, who lived on the Gargano.

Consumed with curiosity the General wanted to know more. One day, incognito, he went to San Giovanni Rotondo. At the monastery he asked to see Padre Pio and was told that if he waited in the corridor that led from the monastery to the sacristy, he would have a chance of seeing him. A few minutes later Padre Pio came along with some of his confrères. When he came to where the general was standing he called out: "Hello, General! We escaped by the skin of our teeth that night didn't we?" The startled general recognized in Padre Pio's face and voice, the Capuchin who had visited him in his tent on a certain night in 1917.

Meeting with Mother Speranza at the Holy Office in Rome

Mother Speranza, foundress of the Ancelle dell'Amore Misericordioso, (Servants of Merciful Love), claimed that Padre Pio came to her every day at the Holy Office in Rome for an entire year. This is such an extraordinary story that one is inclined to dismiss it as fantasy if one did not believe in the Almighty Power of God and the testimony of a woman as saintly as Mother Speranza. She told this to Father Alberto D'Apolito in the course of an interview in February 1970. "Mother," he said to her,

"I am a Capuchin from San Giovanni Rotondo. I don't want to take up your time but I want to ask your prayers for myself and for the glorification of Padre Pio."

Mother Speranza, who was small and bent, raised her eyes and looked at him saying: "I have always prayed for Padre Pio."

"Did you know him?" the priest asked.

"Yes, I saw him often."

"Where? At San Giovanni Rotondo?"

"No, I never went there."

"Then, where did you know him?"

"In Rome!"

"But Mother," the priest said, "Padre Pio only went to Rome once, when he was very young on May 17th, 1917 to accompany his sister who was entering an enclosed order at St. Bridget's convent. You were in Spain at that time. You must be mistaken and confusing Padre Pio with some other Capuchin."

"No," she replied, "I am not mistaken, it really was Padre Pio."

"Where in Rome did you see him?"

"I saw him every day, for a year, at the Holy Office. He wore mittens to cover his wounds. I greeted him, kissed his hand and he spoke with me."

"In what year did you have these daily visits?"

"When I was working at the Holy Office between 1937 and 1939."

"Mother," Father Alberto said, "your story seems very strange and highly improbable. I can hardly believe it."

"Father, I have to tell you that I have never been subject to hallucinations and I would add this to what I have said. A mysterious person used to fly in from Milan. He had a white beard was very ugly and I was afraid of him."

"Who was he?" the priest asked, "A friar?"

"I don't know. Whenever I saw him I was struck with terror and wanted to run away. I had the impression he was some kind of demon!"

"What was his business at the Holy Office?"

"He came to testify against Padre Pio!"

"Mother, please do not be offended if I tell you that I find your story difficult to believe."

Without the slightest sign of resentment Mother Speranza said quietly to Father Alberto: "Father, you can think what you want. I tell you again, I saw Padre Pio, in Rome, every day for a year. I have always prayed for him and now I will pray for his beatification."

"Get rid of that friar!"

In June, 1973, a woman came from Rome to San Giovanni Rotondo to give thanks to Padre Pio for the help he had given her dying husband. She told me what actually happened.

It was discovered that her husband had a malignant tumour. In the hospital he went through every conceivable treatment but without any great hope of a cure. Back at home the sick man became aware of the incurable nature of his illness and got worse day by day. His family had a great devotion to Padre Pio and so began praying to him to come to their assistance.

One day in his room the patient began to cry out in a loud voice: "Get rid of that friar! He tells me to go with him. Chase him away! I do not want to go!" Those around came running and tried to calm him down by telling him there was no friar to be seen. "Why, can't you see him?" the sick man asked, "He is at the foot of my bed." They told him again there was no one there and that he should calm down, which he eventually did. They asked him what the friar looked like. The man replied: "He was a Capuchin with a white beard and he told me he would come back for me on the 5th of February." They showed him a photo of Padre Pio and he recognized him immediately: "Yes, that's he!"

The family intensified their prayers and the sick man appeared to be a little better. He was able to get up and go to church for Mass and Holy Communion and he prayed fervently every day. Suddenly, on February 5th, 1973, he got worse and died peacefully in great serenity.

Padre Pio had kept his promise. He came for him and brought him home to the Lord in the next life.

"Get away from here!"

This next incident happened on a battlefield during World War I. A captain was urging his soldiers to resist enemy attack. At a particular moment, he saw a friar with a pale face and sparkling eyes, who called out to him: "Get away from here, captain. Come to me! Quick! Quick!" Attracted by the face and the voice the captain jumped up and went towards him. He had hardly reached the priest when he heard the terrible explosion of a bomb that had dropped just where he had been standing!

Terror-stricken, he looked in that direction for a moment and then turned round to thank the priest who had saved him but, to his amazement, he was nowhere to be seen. The friar's face, nonetheless, was engraved on his memory.

One day, when he was telling this story to friends, one of them suggested that perhaps the stigmatist at Gargano, Padre Pio, might be the person he saw that day. He set out for San Giovanni Rotondo. Padre Pio had just finished Mass and was putting away the vestments in the sacristy. The captain looked closely at him and cried out: "That's the friar! That is certainly the friar I saw!" He went forward and threw himself at Padre Pio's feet, kissed his hand and, overcome, thanked him.

The priest put his hand on the officer's head and said: "It's not me you should be thanking but Our Lord and the Blessed Virgin."

"I replied that night at the inn."

A young English married couple had serious problems that caused them great distress. One of their friends spoke to them of Padre Pio, who had the stigmata and to whom countless people came in their distress. The couple wrote to him telling him of their situation.

Their letter was not answered. Although they were not well off they decided to go in person to San Giovanni. On their journey they stopped at a cheap hotel in Berne, Switzerland. Their room was in a damp, mouldy attic. It was winter and snowing. They became discouraged and wondered if it was worthwhile to continue on such an arduous and long journey with no guarantee that they would even meet Padre Pio at the end of it!

They were in this perplexed state of mind when, suddenly, a sweet perfume surrounded them and imparted a kind of comfort. They looked in every corner of the room to find out where it came from, but could not find its source. The perfume went just as suddenly as it had come. They asked the innkeeper about this phenomenon but he was at great pains to assure them that no one had spread perfume in their room. The young couple remained intrigued by this incident.

Padre Pio welcomed them as if he had always known them. They reminded him that they had written and he had not replied. "What do you mean, I did not reply? I replied that night at the inn. Did you not smell the perfume?"

Then, suddenly they realized that Padre Pio had come to their help by encouraging them to keep going to San Giovanni Rotondo. He listened to them, helped them solve their problems and the young couple went back to England, happy and at peace.

A guide in the desert

The newspaper, *Il Progresso Italo-Americano,* carried this story in its October 24th, 1949 edition.

Pietro Cadice and his family lived in Rome. His son, Giacomo, was very unhappy at home so ran away and joined the Foreign Legion. When his parents noticed his absence, they notified the police who searched in vain for him. In time, the family of the young runaway received a letter saying he was at the Foreign Legion training camp in Sidi-Bel-Abbes, a training centre in Africa, had signed on for five years and could not come back home until his time was up. His father fell into a depression. He did not know what saint to turn to! A friend persuaded him to go to Padre Pio. Pietro told Padre Pio all that his son had done and begged him to send him back home. After listening attentively, Padre Pio put his hand on Pietro's head and said: "Go and pray! By the third moon your son will return home!"

The following part of the story was told by the son himself, when he returned home on the very date indicated by Padre Pio. The young man explained that one night, when, in a state of fever, he was on guard duty at an advanced post, he saw a friar who came and took him by the hand inviting the soldier to follow him.

They went across the desert for several days and finally reached the coast where they boarded a ship. The friar disappeared and the young man disembarked at Marseille, then went on to Sardinia and finally reached Rome and his family. It is not difficult to imagine everyone's joy at his return!

One puzzle remained, however. Who was the friar who had led the boy through the desert? Pietro showed his son a photo of Padre Pio. With tears in his eyes, the young man immediately recognized the priest as the one who had saved him. Padre Pio had kept his promise.

Padre Pio in California

The United States newspaper *L'Italia e la Voce del Popolo*, edited in San Francisco, California, carried the following story on 3rd March, 1956, by Father Giuseppe G. Tursi, R.C.J., which tells of Padre Pio's presence in the city of Fresno in California, where he cured a sick man.

Bartolomeo Pollina, a Sicilian emigrant, lived for many years in the town of Fresno. He suffered from an incapacitating hernia which became dangerous. The doctors advised him to have an operation as soon as possible but the sick man would not hear of the surgeon's knife!

Through reading he had come to know Padre Pio and the marvels he performed. He hoped that Padre Pio would cure him of his illness before he had to go into surgery. He wrote to the priest, asking him to intercede with the Lord on his behalf. In the reply he was told that Padre Pio was interested in his case, would pray for him and that he should also pray and trust in the Lord.

Time went by and nothing happened. One night, however, just as he was about to retire he heard someone breathing heavily at the foot of his bed. He was afraid for a moment but the rest of the night passed without incident. The next night the same thing happened but this time the breathing came from the side of the bed. The third night he heard the breathing again, at the head of the bed. On the morning after the third day, Mr. Pollina felt two hands working around the area of the hernia to put everything back in its natural position again. He was wide awake and followed this "operation" trembling a little but fully convinced that Padre Pio had come to cure him. He then felt great interior peace. When he got up he felt the affected area and realized he had, in fact, been cured. He was able to take up his full activities again without any fear of hurting himself.

Full of gratitude he wrote to Padre Pio to thank him for this cure and for having heard his prayers. He promised to live a more Christian life. In his reply, Padre Pio told him to thank the Lord and to trust him always.

"I know it better than you!"

In 1949, a church dedicated to the Holy Family was built in Pietrelcina, (Benevent), Padre Pio's birthplace. When the work was finished plans were made for the official opening due to take place on May 20th.

On the eve of this event the Bishop, Mgr. Agostino Mancinelli, was to consecrate the church. The Capuchin Superiors were trying to find a way of having Padre Pio present without creating a commotion among the people. They agreed to keep their idea an absolute secret! However, in spite of their efforts, word got out that Padre Pio was coming! The plan failed and Padre Pio could not go to Pietrelcina. He did not seem to know anything about the opening of the new church.

Later, in the course of a conversation, Father Alberto D'Apolito said to Padre Pio: "Spiritual Father, (a name given to Padre Pio by his confrères), why don't you come some day and see the church. It is very beautiful." Padre Pio replied: "I know it better than you!" "Did you see a photograph of it, perhaps?" Father Alberto asked. "No!" answered Padre Pio, "I went there. I can describe it in great detail. Do you know how many steps there are at the entrance?" Father Alberto had never counted them.

The presence of Padre Pio at Pietrelcina was confirmed in the diary of the Father Provincial at the time, Father Agostino da San Marco in Lamis. One day he said to Padre Pio that he would be absolutely delighted to see a monastery open at Pietrelcina. Padre Pio said to him: "And you will be the Guardian (Superior), when you have finished serving as Provincial." "Will you come to the ceremony?" Father Agostino asked. "Yes," said Padre Pio, "I will be present and at the same time will be here in San Giovanni Rotondo hearing confessions!"

Padre Pio in Uruguay

Mgr. Damiani, Vicar General of the diocese of Salto in Uruguay, wanted to end his days in San Giovanni Rotondo, to be near Padre Pio. He spoke about his desire to Padre Pio but the priest told him that his place was in the diocese of Salto and not in San Giovanni Rotondo. Msgr. Damiani asked Padre Pio then to come and help him at the moment of death. After praying for a moment he agreed to do this.

This is how this promise was kept according to the account of events given by Msgr. Barbieri, Archbishop of Montevideo.

In 1941, Msgr. Alfredo Viola, Archbishop of Salto, was celebrating his priestly jubilee with several other bishops, among them, Archbishop Barbieri. During his sleep he heard someone knock on his bedroom door. Suddenly he was wide awake. A Capuchin came into his room and said to him: "Go to Msgr. Damiani. He is dying." Msgr. Barbieri got up right away, put on some clothes, took the Holy Oils, and with some other priests went to Msgr. Damiani's bedside. He was, in fact, dying but very lucid. After receiving the Sacrament of the Sick he died very peacefully.

On the bedside table Msgr. Barbieri found a piece of paper on which the following words were written in a very shaky hand: "Padre Pio came!" He decided to keep this note so that he could check out the facts on his next trip to Italy.

On April 13th, 1949, taking advantage of the *Ad Limina* visit every bishop makes to the Pope from time to time, he decided to visit Padre Pio. When they met he immediately recognized the Capuchin who had come to his room that night. However, to make quite sure, he questioned Padre Pio about his visit to Uruguay. Padre Pio remained silent, preferring to say nothing. Msgr. Barbieri, afraid that he had perhaps not understood what he was asking, repeated the question but Padre Pio still remained silent.

Msgr. Barbieri realized that the event had really happened, so he said to Padre Pio: "I understand." Padre Pio said to him: "But, of course, you understand!"

"We cannot find Padre Pio!"

A luxury car drew up one day in the square at the monastery of San Giovanni Rotondo. Several grand ladies got out accompanied by a conceited young man who made it quite clear he had come to ridicule Padre Pio. He asked some people nearby where he could find Padre Pio. They told him he would be in the sacristy where he heard confessions. The young man disappeared into the church and went to the sacristy. "Where is Padre Pio?" he demanded to know. He was told the priest had just left to go to the church. He must surely have passed him? "No! I didn't see him." said the young man. "But that's impossible!" he was told. "Padre Pio went out the door you just came through!" The young man and his party were becoming rather annoyed. They asked some Capuchins who were nearby to find Padre Pio. They searched everywhere but in vain, Padre Pio was nowhere to be found!

After a fruitless search they apologized to the group, declaring that they were puzzled by his absence. The young man was really annoyed and said: "He must have gone out! Where is he likely to have gone?" The priests told him: "Padre Pio never leaves the monastery! We have no idea where he might be!"

More furious than ever, and feeling extremely let down and frustrated, the young man and the ladies went back to their car, fuming, and drove away. Those standing around saw the car disappear but what did they see when they turned round? Padre Pio was standing there! They told him how they had searched everywhere for him without success. "I was here all the time." he told them. "I walked back

and forth in front of you but you did not see me!"
Then he went into the church to hear confessions.

A thwarted air-raid

During World War II a general at the American
base near Bari heard that the Germans had an arms
depot somewhere around San Giovanni Rotondo. He
planned an air raid to destroy the depot and led the
squadron on this mission. Near the target he saw
a friar ascend into the air with his hands out-
stretched! The planes could not respond to com-
mands and so, dropping their bombs in the forest,
they turned round and went back to base.

The general could not understand. He talked
about the incident to the officers and pilots but no
one could come up with a reasonable explanation.
Who was this friar who had obstructed their mission and disabled the planes' communication sys-
tem? What a mystery!

One day, he heard someone speak of a Capuchin
called Padre Pio who lived on Mt. Gargano and
worked miracles. Suspecting that this was the monk
who had thwarted the bombardment, he went to San
Giovanni Rotondo to see for himself.

The priest came towards him, put his hand on
his shoulder and said: "Ah! So you are the one who
wanted to kill us all!" The astounded general was
won over by the eyes and personality of Padre Pio.
He became a Catholic and a friend and follower of
Padre Pio until the end of his days.

It is worth noting an additional and curious detail. When Padre Pio spoke to the general he used

the Benevent dialect, yet the American heard every word in perfect English!

Padre Pio at Maglie (Lecce)

The father of one of the Capuchins at the Maglie (Lecce) monastery was seriously ill, the victim of a disease of the spinal cord. He was unable to walk and finally became bedridden. It was said he would never walk again.

His son, who knew Padre Pio and had great confidence in him, wrote to him asking him to intercede urgently with the Lord for his sick father who was slowly dying. Padre Pio wrote back assuring the Capuchin that he was praying for his father and urging him to trust in God.

The days went on and the illness took its relentless course. One afternoon, the sick man suddenly saw a bearded friar near his bed who spoke to him: "You are suffering! Suffer with patience!" The same thing happened the next day and the day after, and for seven days more but the sick man's condition did not change. On the contrary, it became worse! On the tenth day it was thought that he should receive the Sacrament of the Sick. That afternoon the same friar reappeared saying: "Look here now! That's enough!"

From that moment the illness subsided and the sick man felt better. Eventually he was completely cured. He was able to take up his life again and go back to his work in the fields.

His son understood that Padre Pio had been part of God's providential plan in all this, and he wrote to thank him.

The blaspheming potter

An old proverb says: *Better to light a candle than curse the dark!* Curses had been plentiful for some time around a potter from Torre Maggiore because he could not get his furnace started due to the sirocco. He was hopping mad! He was losing money and his living because he could not fire his pottery. He had almost exhausted his litany of swear words, curses and blasphemies when he thought he would add Padre Pio's name to the list! Suddenly a friar came up behind him and said: "Peace be with you!" Peace was the last thing on his mind! He told the friar that he would have no peace as long as the cursed wind kept him from using his furnace. Padre Pio repeated: "Peace be with you!"

The friar sat down on a crate and with a gesture asked for some fire. Seeing the potter beside himself with rage, the priest added: "I will light it myself!" The potter retorted with: "Perhaps you are like that Padre Pio who works miracles for simpletons?" The priest replied: "I am Padre Pio!" The fire lit up immediately and the potter just had time to hear the friar say before he disappeared: "Don't be afraid, Michael, and stop swearing!"

Orders from a loudspeaker

During the turmoil that followed the collapse of Fascism in Italy, a young woman who was a follower of Padre Pio, was unjustly denounced as a "collaborator". She was arrested by partisans and condemned to death after a summary trial. Although she was completely innocent, she had no way of proving this. In great distress during this terrible trial she invoked Padre Pio in her heart, asking him to come to her assistance. Meanwhile, she was taken down the road to the place of execution. Suddenly, just as the execution squad were about to cross a road, a column of tanks, ambulances and troops passed through coming from the south en route for the north. The partisans had to wait until this convoy passed through and the young woman knew that when the last vehicle passed she would be on her way again to be shot.

She called all the more on Padre Pio's help. The military vehicles took much longer than expected to go through and some of the partisans grew tired of waiting, so they went away leaving only their leader who stayed doggedly at his post.

In the meantime some friends of the young girl heard of her predicament and set about getting evidence to prove her innocence to the authorities concerned.

Just as she started out again on the road to her death, a car drew up alongside and a man leaned out saying she had been freed and offered her a lift home!

When she got home she found hooligans were looting and vandalizing her house. They thought she had been killed and were helping themselves to her possessions. Her terrified sister could do nothing but watch. Suddenly, a very loud voice, like a loud-speaker, cried out twice: "That's enough! That's enough!" At this, the looters left everything and ran.

The young woman attributed this, as well as her liberation to Padre Pio's intervention. As soon as she could, she went to San Giovanni Rotondo to thank Padre Pio. The priest welcomed her and, smiling, said: "What confidence you have, my daughter! If you only knew how you had me running for you!"

A strange way to get out

When news of Padre Pio's stigmata got out people flocked to him out of curiosity or for confession. This influx of people, coming from all over, grew daily and meant a great deal of apostolic work not only for Padre Pio but for the other friars as well. The church was too small to hold such crowds especially in the summer when there was great danger of people being crushed.

One day in summer, the church was so packed that the atmosphere was suffocating. Some people in the crowd were near to passing out. The entrance was blocked by the crowds. Padre Pio decided to leave the confessional to go outside. He did this in a rather unusual way! Without anyone seeing him he went through the throng by an odd route. Everyone saw that he was no longer in the confessional but no one had seen him leave.

Father Agostino, who was Padre Pio's former Provincial and spiritual director, asked him how he had moved through a crowd that was packed together like sardines. "I walked on their shoulders!" Padre Pio replied. "And what about their heads, Father Agostino asked, "Did they not get in the way?" "No Father, they were like pebbles under my feet!"

A pervading perfume

Giuseppe Onofrio worked in the Tax Department. In 1942 he was at the office in Rieti and then transferred to Lucera in the Province of Foggia. He had been an atheist since his youth and only gone to church to get married. On this occasion he went to confession, made his First Communion and received the sacrament of Confirmation. After that he led a peaceful Christian life.

At Lucera he heard people speak of Padre Pio and the wonderful things he did. He wanted to meet this friar. In April, 1943 an opportunity came up and he went to the little Capuchin church at San Giovanni Rotondo.

When he saw Padre Pio and attended his Mass, something stirred within him and he wanted to go to confession. When he came face to face with the priest he was asked a question to which he could not reply. Padre Pio told him to go to the church and wait there until he was called. He had to wait a long time. He began to lose patience and was about to leave when he was called and the confession began. Throughout this time Padre Pio held his right hand. The confession ended and Onofrio left but he noticed a perfume coming from the hand Padre Pio had held. This lasted for two months.

He had occasion to visit Padre Pio again. This time he asked the priest's advice on whether or not he should ask for a transfer. Padre Pio said he could, but he would encounter many difficulties. Onofrio, nevertheless, asked for a change and had to move about often from one place to another. He noticed, however, that through all these moves Padre Pio's perfume remained on his right hand. He finally got the post he wanted and settled in Palermo.

On the 18th of December 1944, he came again to see Padre Pio, this time with all his family. They came to thank the priest and to go to confession. The first to go into the confessional was his little daughter. Without ever having seen her before he said: "Your dad is happy now isn't he?" Then it was her little brother's turn. Padre Pio had never met him either. He asked: "What are you doing here? You are already in a state of grace. Go, and remain that way forever!"

Behind the Bishop

Bishop D'Indico, from Florence, had a sister who had contracted paratyphoid A and B and was in a coma, in a desperate condition. Her parents had written to Padre Pio asking him to intercede with the Lord, on their behalf, so that their daughter might be cured. On the 20th of July 1921, Msgr. D'Indico, her brother, was alone in his office when he had the feeling that someone was standing behind him. He turned round just in time to see a friar walking away. He thought of Padre Pio and was afraid.

He quickly left his office and went out. While walking, he met one of his chaplains and told him what had happened. The priest did not believe the story and thought the Bishop was suffering from hallucinations brought on by the stress of his sister's impending death. To take his mind off things he invited the Bishop to go for a walk with him.

On their return to the bishop's house they were called by the sick woman who had suddenly come out of the coma. She told them what had happened. Padre Pio had come and said to her: "Do not be afraid! Tomorrow your fever will disappear and in a few days there will be no trace of the illness in your body." She told him she thought he was a saint who had come to heal her. She commended her husband and daughter to his prayers, then asked permission to kiss his hand. Padre Pio held out his hands, with the stigmata, and taking his leave said: "I leave you with the memory of my visit of July 20th, 1921."

In a few days the woman was completely recovered, as Padre Pio had predicted.

Other cases of Padre Pio's power of bilocation

In July 1921, Padre Pio went to the bedside of the dying Msgr. Paolo Schinosi, Bishop of Benevent, who had ordained him priest on August 10th, 1910.

Cleonice Morcaldi relates that one day, Padre Pio visited her sister in a convent in Rome, through bilocation and, in the same way, went to America on Christmas night to see her father, Grazio Forgione.

Colonel Russo of Caserta tells that during World War II he was a prisoner of war in a camp in India. Padre Pio came to visit the prisoners every night. When the war was over many of these men, on coming home, went to San Giovanni Rotondo to thank the priest. Padre Pio knew each and everyone of them!

Don Orione, considered to be a saint, says that he saw Padre Pio in St. Peter's, in Rome, at the time of the canonization of St. Teresa of the Child Jesus.

Gaetano Pavone, an engineer, was a gunner in the American Air Force. While flying over Mt. Gargano between the lakes of Verano and Lesina he saw Padre Pio appear before him covering the whole sky! For a long time, he did not want to talk about this in case he would be laughed at, but he told his wife on September 23rd, 1968, the day Padre Pio died. As might be expected, she passed on this story.

It is also recorded that Padre Pio went to Budapest and brought Cardinal Mindszenty everything he needed to celebrate Mass when he took refuge in the American Embassy.

It is also known that Padre Pio celebrated Mass for Sisters in a convent in Czechoslovakia. The Sisters were so convinced of the reality of his presence that, after the celebration, they went to thank him and offer him a cup of coffee. Imagine their surprise when they could not find the priest who had, meanwhile, disappeared!

All these accounts of bilocation are certainly not the only times Padre Pio used this power. He was very careful not to divulge the gifts given him by God. Here we have reported only those we have heard about because of the unusual circumstances surrounding them.

6

THE PATH TO HEALTH

Many came to Padre Pio in his lifetime, and still more do today, to ask him to intercede with God for better health.

He was very careful to point out, and sometimes with characteristic vigour, that it was the Lord who was responsible for the cures effected, not he. His role was simply to pray for those in suffering. However, the fact remains that when Padre Pio prayed, the Lord cured.

The list of healings would be too long to include here. We have limited ourselves to those which were the most striking in order to show clearly that for many unfortunate people, Padre Pio was their path to health according to the Plan of God.

At a particular moment, Padre Pio wondered: "The Lord grants spectacular cures to many people but what of those who are not part of this divine plan? Have they to bear this cross of ill-health? Can't something be done for them too?"

This gave Padre Pio the idea to take on the huge task of building the *Casa Sollievo della Sofferenza*, (the House for the Relief of Suffering). In his mind, this was not to be simply a hospital but a house, a safe haven for his brothers, bearing the image of Christ, who would be cared for as if they were Christ Himself. Jesus had, in fact, said: "Whatever you do to the least of my brothers, you do unto me."

This "house" was to be a model in all aspects: human, Christian, medical, scientific and technical. To launch this great enterprise, Padre Pio called on everyone to help and offerings came from all over the world. It is interesting, however, to know how the first "financial stone" was laid.

When news got out that Padre Pio was building the *Casa*, a little old woman came up to him and offered a small gold coin. Padre Pio saw how poor this woman was and said to her: "Thank you! But you should keep this for yourself. You need it!"

"No! Father," she replied, "take it!"

He insisted that she keep it: "You can't take the bread out of your mouth! Do as I say and keep it for your own needs." The woman had a qualm about this and felt mortified: "You are right, Father," she said, "This is too small!" Padre Pio was very moved by this and said to her: "Please, give it to me and may God bless you!"

When the time came to consider the financing of the *Casa*'s construction, Padre Pio said to the Management Committee: "I will start it off!" He gave them the little gold coin. There is certainly an echo of the Gospel here!

The dead baby in the suitcase

A six-month-old baby was in a state of bad health that brought him close to death. The poor mother,

110

who had great faith, thought she might save the baby by taking him to Padre Pio so that he might intercede with God for a cure.

It was a long distance to travel but, full of courage, she took the train. During the journey, due either to the child's serious condition or the rigours of travel, he died. The desolate mother wrapped the body in some clothes and put it in a fibre suitcase.

On arrival at the church she ran up the steps and, suitcase in hand, took her place in the line of women waiting for confession. When her turn came, she threw herself at Padre Pio's feet and crying pitifully, opened the case.

Doctor Sanguinetti, a convert and Padre Pio's right-hand man at the *Casa Sollievo della Sofferenza*, was present at this incident. He realized right away that, even if the baby had not died of the illness he had, he most certainly would have died of suffocation, being closed in the case for so long. At the sight of this Padre Pio paled and was gripped by emotion. He raised his eyes to heaven, prayed for a few moments and then turned abruptly to the mother saying: "Why are you crying so loud? Can't you see that your son is sleeping?" It was true. The baby was now sleeping peacefully!

The happiness of this mother was beyond description as were her cries of joy and those of everyone who saw what had happened.

Sight without pupils

Can a person see without pupils? It is not humanly possible. However, there is someone still living today who was born without pupils and who now sees. From the moment Padre Pio made the Sign of the Cross on her eyes she began to see and even to this day she still has no pupils! Her name is Gemma Di Giorgi. Born on Christmas night, 1939, her parents noticed she had strange eyes. Something was missing. The village doctor consulted two specialists in Palermo, Doctor Cucco and Dr. Contino. These men examined the little girl and discovered she had no pupils. Their prognosis was that she would be blind for the rest of her life because no one can see without pupils.

The parents were devastated by this news. They, nevertheless, trusted Divine Providence and often prayed in the Chapel of our Lady at the church. One day they had a visit from an aunt, a nun, who advised them to contact Padre Pio. The little girl's grandmother was quite prepared to accompany her to San Giovanni Rotondo. She asked the nun to write to Padre Pio and commend the little blind girl to his prayers. One night the nun dreamt of the priest and he asked her: "Where is this Gemma for whom you bombard me with prayers?" Still in the dream, the nun brought Gemma to him and he made the Sign of the Cross on her eyes.

The next day she received a letter from Padre Pio. It read: "Dear daughter, I assure you of my prayers for the little one. Best wishes!" Impressed by the coincidence between the dream and Padre Pio's reply to her letter, she urged the little girl's grandmother to take her right away to San Giovanni Rotondo. The old lady had no need to be told twice so she took her granddaughter and set out without delay. On the train Gemma told her she thought she could see something but the grandmother did not believe her because no one can see without pupils.

On arriving, Gemma and her grandmother went quickly to the church and to Padre Pio for confession. The little girl had not yet made her First Communion and this seemed a good opportunity for her to receive Communion from the hands of Padre Pio himself.

The grandmother told the little girl to ask Padre Pio, in the confessional, to pray that she might see, but she forgot. When Gemma came to him, Padre Pio put his hands on her eyes and made the Sign of the Cross.

After confession the grandmother asked Gemma if she had thought to petition Padre Pio for her sight. The little girl told her she had forgotten to do that. The woman was very upset at this and began to cry. She then went off to find Padre Pio herself and intercede for Gemma's cure. Padre Pio said to her: "Have confidence, my daughter. You must not make Gemma cry and you must not worry about her. Gemma sees, you know!"

The little girl received her First Holy Communion with Padre Pio, who after giving her the host, again made the Sign of the Cross on her eyes. On the day set for their return journey they took the train home. The little girl noticed that her sight was getting better and better to the point of being normal.

At Cosenza, the grandmother became ill and had to stay in hospital for a few days. Before leaving she took Gemma to an oculist who was absolutely astounded to discover that she could see perfectly well although she had no pupils!

A few months later Gemma went with her parents to a specialist in Perugia. He also attested to the fact that she could see normally even without pupils and admitted that there was no human explanation for this.

Gemma still sees like this. She lives in her village but, from time to time, she leaves it to tell her wonderful story!

A rigid leg bends

On the 26th of June, 1946, Giuseppe Canaponi, a railwayman, was riding his motorcycle to work when a truck hit him. He was taken to the hospital with a broken left leg and other more critical injuries. His life was saved but his leg remained rigid.

Canaponi could not accept this and did everything to recover the use of his leg. He went round many reputable orthopaedic hospitals but to no avail. He despaired of ever being well again. He was in full vigour and had a wife and son to support, yet he could only take a few steps with the help of two sticks. In his most depressed moments he became angry and would insult everybody and swear. Then he would regret his behaviour, calm himself and get back to normal.

One day his wife spoke to him of Padre Pio and suggested that he go to him. At first, Canaponi reacted violently and spoke against the priest. In the end, he allowed himself to be persuaded and set out for San Giovanni Rotondo with his wife and child. At the church he asked for Padre Pio. As soon as the priest saw Canaponi he said: "You curse and swear a lot, you insult everyone and get upset with yourself!" Canaponi replied: "Yes, Father, I do." "But afterwards," the priest went on, "you are sorry and go to your room to pray." Then Padre Pio began to list all the sins the man had committed in his life. Canaponi was quite astounded and asked the priest how he could know all this when they had only just met and then he asked him: "Father, pray to the Lord for me that he might rid me of this terrible fault." Padre Pio replied: "You must be strong, otherwise it is useless for the Lord to give you his grace."

Without having noticed it, Canaponi was kneeling before Padre Pio, in spite of his rigid leg! On getting up he noticed that the stiffness had gone. He put his sticks under his arm and went into the church where his wife and son were waiting. When his wife saw him walking normally, she could not believe her eyes but their son convinced her because he had seen his father kneeling and getting up again.

Back at their hotel, Canaponi wanted to make sure his leg was really cured. He put a cushion on the floor and knelt down and got up again several times. Everything was normal again! The next day he went back to the church to thank Padre Pio. "I did not cure you." Padre Pio said, "Thank the Lord, and Him alone for this grace."

Back home Canaponi was submitted repeatedly to orthopaedic tests. The wonderful thing is that the X-Ray results showed the leg to be still rigid yet he was enjoying complete mobility!

A doctor turns to God

Doctor Antonio Scarparo, who practiced medicine in Padua, discovered one day that he had cancer. There was no doubt about it. He, better than anyone, recognized the symptoms.

His brother Giovanni, who often went to see Padre Pio, told him about his brother's case and asked what could be done. Padre Pio advised an operation. The doctor had the operation in 1960 and everything seemed quite normal again. However in May, 1962 the illness reappeared. An X-Ray taken by Dr. Bruno Bonomini revealed "a lung infection caused by testicular seminoma". He had three months to live!

When Padre Pio heard this he said: "He must take care of himself." The sick man came to San Giovanni Rotondo and showed the X-Rays to Padre Pio who blessed them. Dr. Antonio begged him: "Obtain this one grace for me! I have three children!" Padre Pio replied: "That is so sad!"

The doctor went back to Padua while his brother remained in San Giovanni Rotondo to plead his cause with Padre Pio. "Father," he said, "the doctors have given my brother only three months to live!" Padre Pio replied: "Don't worry so much! That's what *they* say!" Then the following dialogue took place between Padre Pio and Giovanni Scarparo:

— "Father, you have said that to obtain this grace one must have faith. I am asking you for this faith."

— "Faith comes through good works."

— "Father, there are no drugs to help my brother but just one thought from you and he will be cured."

— "Yes, if God wants it."

— "But it was Jesus who said: 'If you have faith the size of a mustard seed you can say to this mountain: Move!' and to this sycamore: 'Be uprooted and go plant yourself in the sea.' "

— "And do you have this faith?"

— "No! I don't but *you* do!"

— "But if you do not have this faith how can you ask this grace of the Lord?"

— "I don't know if I have it and even if I do have it I don't know how much!"

— "I understand! I understand! You have even less than a grain of mustard seed!"

While this conversation was taking place between Padre Pio and Giovanni Scarparo, Dr. Bonomini, in Padua, was studying the results of the X-Rays, over and over again. He began to realize that there was no trace of the cancer!

When Giovanni heard this, he went back to Padre Pio to tell him. The priest simply said: "Let us thank the Lord!" Scarparo added: "Father, I made a vow, that if my brother was cured I would give up smoking." "Well," said Padre Pio, "stop right now!" Dr. Antonio Scarparo was completely and definitively cured.

A cripple is healed

One day, in 1919, a beggar, who was also crippled, came to the Capuchin Monastery door at San Giovanni Rotondo. His name was Francesco Viscio, but he was nicknamed Santaredda. He was forty-three years old. An illness contracted in the early months of his life had left him with his feet turned inward so badly he needed crutches to walk. When he did not have these, he crawled about on all fours.

The children of San Giovanni Rotondo made fun of him and laughed at him. They would take away his crutches so that he had to crawl on his hands and knees. All he could do was yell at them.

Every day he went to the monastery for something to eat and there was always plenty even when the number of beggars had increased as was the case on that day in 1919. On that particular day, Viscio was tired of such a life and seeing Padre Pio go by called out to him: "Father, grant me a favour!" The priest stopped, looked at him intently and said in dialect: "Throw away your crutches!" The unfortunate man did not quite understand and was hesitant. Again Padre Pio called even more loudly to him: "Throw away your crutches!" Torn between incredulity and hope he tried to get up, and succeeded! He did it again and realized that he was able to walk normally.

The man was overcome with joy and astonishment as was everyone around who witnessed the incident. This was the beginning of a new life for Viscio. This lasted for several years, then he died.

Antonio Egidio, one of Padre Pio's spiritual sons, on recalling this case asked the priest: "When a cripple like Santaredda goes to heaven, tell me, what happens to him?" Padre Pio remained silent and pensive for a moment then, with a start, he pointed to the ceiling and said: "Look! This is what happens!" Egidio looked up and saw an opening in the sky which revealed Viscio in Paradise, resplendent in glory. This lasted but an instant and then vanished. When Egidio turned to Padre Pio, he also had disappeared!

God's plans take time

Padre Pio told Mr. & Mrs. Pennisi that God had a plan for the cure of their sick daughter Maria, but they did not have the patience to follow it step by step. Their daughter was cured, all the same, but she suffered the consequences of her parents' impatience.

The girl was born in New York but went with her parents when they returned to Italy to settle in Pietrelcina, (Benevent), the home village of Padre Pio. Soon afterwards, in 1922, she contracted tuberculosis. At that time this disease was relentless. She coughed continually and suffered from pain in her right shoulder.

The parents did everything in their power for the cure of their child but to no avail. They took her to Naples for examinations by excellent doctors, among them, the saintly Joseph Moscati. After sounding her thoroughly, he had to agree with his colleagues that the little girl had an incurable type of TB and would die very soon. Her parents brought her back to Pietrelcina and did everything they could to alleviate her suffering.

One day, her father decided to take her to Padre Pio. As his wife could not come that day he went with a sister-in-law. Padre Pio had never heard of the sick girl nor had he ever met her, yet he said to her: "You are Maria Pennesi, are you sick? No, you are in better health than I am!" And he put his hand on her shoulder. At this point the father thought it his duty to let the priest know that his daughter was seriously ill and that he had brought her to him for a cure. Padre Pio replied: "Don't worry! I will take care of her!"

They went back to the hotel and the next day the girl said she felt better and wanted to go to the church at the monastery to receive Holy Communion from Padre Pio. She did this for eight consecutive days. The father then decided it was time to go back to Pietrelcina because his daughter had to go to school. Nonetheless, before leaving he went to ask Padre Pio's advice on the matter. Padre Pio advised him: "She should go back to school only after the Christmas break." "But, Father," the man said, "you can cure her just as easily from a distance." "No!" said Padre Pio, "you must leave her here at San Giovanni. I want to keep an eye on her!"

Mr. Pennesi did not want to take this advice so he took his daughter home. A few days later the girl developed pleurisy. When he was told of this, Padre Pio exclaimed: "Had she remained at San Giovanni, this would never have happened!"

Her parents called in doctors who were undecided as to whether they should drain the pleura or not. The child was in critical condition and they feared the worst. At this point a woman, who had been to see Padre Pio, arrived with some articles belonging to the priest. She asked to be allowed to rub the little girl's body with one of them. The parents consented and the little girl fell into a peaceful sleep. When she woke up, the fever which had been as high as 40° had subsided to 37° and Maria felt well. The doctor who attended her checked the temperature again and again but it stayed at 37°. The astounded doctor had to acknowledge that the fever had gone and his patient was cured. "We must also believe in miracles!" he said.

The parents wrote to Padre Pio telling him of the cure and asking if it was time for their daughter to go back to school. "She must wait another twelve days," he told them. This time they obeyed!

In spite of missing fifty-three days of school, due to her illness, the girl came first in her class. When she and her parents went to thank Padre Pio, he said to her: "Thank the Lord who rid you of your cough and cured you again this time. He alone is to be thanked and no one else."

"Surgical intervention is unnecessary!"

Padre Pio said this when he knew God wanted to heal someone. This was the case for Palma Mannelli.

In June 1940, she experienced sudden violent pains in the abdomen followed by internal bleeding. She was taken by emergency ambulance to the hospital where the doctors diagnosed cancer of the womb.

Palma went to Florence for a series of radium treatments. A month later she saw some positive results but she wondered if they were just temporary. The doctors discharged her and asked her to return a few months later for a checkup.

Palma went back home, but unfortunately the cancer reappeared leaving her with two options. She could either go back for more radium treatments or have the womb removed. She had a daughter,

Liliane, who, one night, dreamt that Padre Pio repeatedly told her: "Your mother will get well and she will get well completely!"

As Palma had been advised not to travel she asked her husband to go to Padre Pio and plead on her behalf for a cure. He made the trip and spoke twice to Padre Pio about his wife's illness. Padre Pio reassured him telling him she must take the necessary treatment but on no account should she undergo an operation: "Above all!" he said, "No surgeon's knife!"

At this precise moment the woman detected the mysterious perfume, characteristic of Padre Pio. That night her daughter had another dream. She saw Padre Pio praying before an altar and holding a gold key to his heart. He said to her: "You are not sleeping well are you?" Then after giving her Holy Communion he led her to a table in the church where there were several pictures of the statue of Our Lady of Grace in the monastery at San Giovanni Rotondo.

Palma returned to Florence for her checkup and underwent extensive examinations by doctors and professors from the University. There was no trace of the cancer! She realized she had been completely and definitively cured.

"Come! Come! There's nothing wrong with you!"

In July 1933, Alessandro Galeoti was seized with excruciating stomach pains which not only affected his breathing but prevented him from keeping down food except for a few sips of syrup and soft drinks.

The family doctor and some excellent specialists could not find the cause of the illness although they ruled out an ulcer or tumour. The sick man was also unable to sleep.

Alessandro had heard of Padre Pio and wanted to go to him and ask his intercession with the Lord for a cure. His mother went with him and they were greeted warmly by Padre Pio who told them to come back to see him in the afternoon. They went back to the hotel, but the young man's condition worsened. With great effort he went back to the monastery to keep his afternoon appointment.

When Padre Pio saw him he went to him, took his hand and pressed it between his own two wounded hands and asked: "Where does it hurt?" "Father, the pain is here," said the young man, pointing to the spot. "I'm afraid I might have a malignant tumour." "Come! Come! There's nothing wrong with you!" At that moment, Alessandro sensed a kind of rupture inside his body and he felt much better. His condition improved until he returned to full health and from that time felt no more pain.

"When the bells ring, you will be healed!"

The following incident took place in 1925 at San Giovanni Rotondo. At the beginning of Holy Week, Mrs. Paolina Preziosi came down with severe bronchitis which developed into pneumonia. The local doctor was called immediately. When he arrived he quickly saw that nothing could be done for her. This situation was particularly sad as her death would leave behind five orphans. Her friends and acquaintances, who loved her very much and admired her for the Christian example she gave everyone, went to the monastery and told Padre Pio about Paolina's situation. They begged him to pray to the Lord for her cure.

He listened to them attentively and said: "Tell her not to be afraid because she will rise with the Lord." This meant she would be cured on Holy Saturday when the bells would ring out again after the silence of Holy Week.

During the night of Good Friday, when she was praying God to cure her for the sake of her children, Padre Pio appeared to her and said: "Don't be scared or afraid, creature of God. Hold onto faith and hope, for tomorrow when the bells ring, you will be cured."

But contrary to these assurances, Mrs. Preziosi went into a coma. Those around her thought the end was near and began thinking of the funeral arrangements. However, those who had told Padre Pio about her the first time had confidence that things would work out. They went back up to the monastery to tell him what was happening and to ask again for his prayers. Padre Pio listened to them, prayed and then went to the confessional.

A little later he was told that the pastor had come to give the Sacrament of the Sick to the dying woman. Padre Pio went to the altar to begin his Mass. When the bells rang out to announce the Lord's Resurrection, Paolina suddenly shuddered a little and felt her strength return. She got out of bed where she had been in a coma and seemed driven by a mysterious force. To the utter astonishment of those around her, of her neighbours and the whole of San Giovanni Rotondo she was completely cured! The grace of the Resurrection had come to her house and to her five children.

Someone went to bring the good news to Padre Pio and added: "Perhaps God wanted this woman to be with him but now she has come back to earth!" The priest replied: "It is also beautiful to be exiled from Paradise because of love."

An atheist doctor is cured

At one time, in San Giovanni Rotondo, everyone knew Dr. Francesco Ricciardi. He had been a doctor for some thirty years and devoted himself completely and generously to the care of the sick.

He was a frank and honest man, but completely closed to things supernatural and had never crossed the threshold of a church. He relied completely on science and considered the spiritual and its manifestations as products of the imagination or fanaticism. He had a strong dislike of Padre Pio, whom he considered to be a dangerous obstacle to the spread of modern knowledge. The people, however, loved the doctor, because he was dedicated to the care of the sick and was full of compassion.

He grew old, as we all do, and he began to feel the weight of the years. He also had a serious illness which concerned him greatly and caused him severe stomach pains.

In February 1931, he began to suspect he was gravely ill and sought the opinion of his colleagues. They diagnosed stomach cancer. The doctor had no illusions about the deadly nature of his illness. He knew he was inexorably condemned to death, but did not know when this would happen. As he did not have the gift of faith, his sufferings were all the harder to bear.

It was winter, and an icy wind mixed with sleet blew on Mt. Gargano. In spite of this, people came to see how he was and bring him the support of their affection and gratitude. One of them had the idea of bringing the pastor to him in case he would be more open to the spiritual. When he saw the priest Dr. Ricciardi ordered to throw him out and the priest had to leave. It was then thought that maybe Padre Pio would succeed better, even if the doctor had been hostile to him in the past. Padre Pio was asked to come to the doctor's bedside. The priest had not left the monastery for ten years but on this occasion he went out. The first thing that happened as he entered the room was that his mysterious perfume filled the air, taking over from the bad smell caused by the dying man's disease. He accepted Padre Pio and the notion of the supernatural!

Padre Pio heard his confession, gave him absolution and his spirit was renewed. To the astonishment of the sick man and those around him, his cancer disappeared and he was restored to full health and filled with a joy he had never known before.

When the people heard about these wonders they were more than happy because not only had their beloved doctor been cured but he had also received the gift of faith.

It happened in a flash!

To save their little girl, who was so gravely ill that the doctors had given up hope, a mother and father went to see Padre Pio to ask his prayers for a cure. They arrived on a Friday. Padre Pio could not receive them because on that day he suffered more than usual from the stigmata and had to stay in bed. The poor parents, anguished by the state of their child, did everything possible to see the priest, but in vain.

In great distress they went home without fulfilling the purpose of their visit, *or so they thought!* Someone, however, had told Padre Pio of their plight and by using his power of bilocation he went to the little girl immediately and cured her.

The distraught parents, knowing nothing about this, thought they would find their daughter dying. They were completely surprised when they reached home to see their child run out to greet them, happy and in perfect health! "What did you do to get Padre Pio to visit me so quickly?" the little girl asked. "You had hardly arrived at San Giovanni Rotondo when he came to cure me!"

It was God's Will that this child be cured, so Padre Pio, through his gift of bilocation, arrived where he was needed, like a flash of lightning.

Padre Pio's perfume cures a cancer

In October 1949, Maria Rosaria Galiano, who lived in Naples, felt a disturbing pain in her abdomen. After a thorough examination Dr. Battiloro advised her to have her womb tissues tested. Unfortunately this revealed the presence of an adenocarcinoma. This was terrible news for Rosaria and her family because they knew that this was an incurable cancer and would, sooner or later, lead to her death. What were they to do? Attempt an operation perhaps? This would not solve anything but merely put off the fatal hour. Rosaria decided to have the operation with the expected result. She felt some relief initially but then the cancer reappeared with all its painful consequences: her pains came back and her condition became worse.

Her daughter, Rita, had heard about all the good that Padre Pio did for the sick, so she contacted him, first by telephone and then sent two letters explaining her mother's condition in detail. The sick woman was in the final stages of the illness and there was little hope of saving her. In spite of this and the scepticism of the doctors and those around her, Rita went on believing in Padre Pio.

On the evening of April 29th, 1950, her mother told her she had smelt a strong perfume in her room and thinking Rita had sprinkled eau de Cologne, she scolded her. Rita thought her mother was delirious and assured her she had not done anything of the sort. Her mother insisted that there was a perfume in her room. It lasted for two consecutive days. Rita began to think that this might be the mysterious perfume of Padre Pio, and her hope of a cure grew stronger. On the third day Rosaria felt better and began to sleep, then she started to eat and digest normally and her suffering ended.

She was examined by two doctors. They had to admit, to their surprise, that the cancer had disappeared. After having gone to thank Padre Pio, Rosaria took up a normal life again. The perfume had gone to the very roots of the disease.

Cured in her sleep

The superior of *L'Escuela Taller Medella Milagrosa*, Montevideo, (America), Mother Teresa Salvadores, was dying of stomach cancer and complications associated with it. She was bedridden and could do nothing for herself. Her Sisters had to attend to her every need.

They had heard of Padre Pio and sent him a touching letter begging him to intercede with God that their Superior might be cured because they loved her very much and did not want to lose her. Mother Teresa was being kept alive with morphine. On the day her letter probably arrived at San Giovanni Rotondo her state became so bad that even the morphine had no effect and death was not far away.

That same day, a relative of Mgr. Damiani, Vicar General of the Diocese of Salto, (Uruguay), to whom Padre Pio had given one of his mittens, arrived at the convent. She suggested that it be applied to the ailing parts of Mother Teresa's body. They placed the mitten, first of all, on her side, where there was a swelling the size of a closed fist and then on the throat, which was tightening up, causing suffocation. She went to sleep after these applications and dreamt that Padre Pio appeared to her, touched her side and breathed on her mouth.

Three hours later Mother Teresa woke up and to everyone's amazement, asked for her clothes, got out of bed, dressed, then went to the chapel to pray. At midday she went to the refectory with her community and ate a hearty meal! All her afflictions had gone and she felt perfectly healthy.

Six months after this sudden and inexplicable cure she was examined by three doctors, among them, a professor from the University of Montevideo. They had to admit that all the stenocardiac symptoms had gone and that Mother Teresa was in excellent health even if the aortic lesion had not changed. Padre Pio had cured the Superior but had left this mysterious sign for the doctors to discuss among themselves!

He ran away from the hospital

Savinio Greco, an ardent militant Communist, lived in the town of Cerignola. It was discovered that he had a brain tumour. He fell into a state of great dejection. He was, first of all, hospitalized in Bari and then moved to Milan where the doctors wanted to attempt difficult surgery. During the night the sick man dreamt that Padre Pio came to him, touched his head and said: "In time you will be cured."

When Savinio woke up he felt cured and wanted to leave the hospital but the doctors did not believe his story and insisted on going through with the operation. The only option left to Savinio was to run away from the hospital. He was caught in Bari and, after some analysis, was put back in the hospital there, where he had first been examined. However, before taking him to the operating room the doctors wanted to be sure that there was a tumour so they examined him again. They had to concede that there was no trace of it! Savinio Greco was able to leave the hospital. Being an honest man, he wanted to pay his bill but the doctors would not take his money saying that they had not done anything.

Savinio went home and then on to San Giovanni Rotondo to thank Padre Pio and to tell him that he would be giving up his communist activities. In the church he was overwhelmed again by an excruciating headache and he fainted with the pain. He was picked up and revived and taken to Padre Pio. The poor man beseeched the priest: "Father, I have five children and I am seriously ill! Save me! Save my family!" Padre Pio replied: "I am not God or even Jesus. I am a priest like other priests, no more no less. I cannot perform miracles." Then deeply moved with pity for the situation of this unfortunate man, he began to pray and as he did so the strong perfume of violets came from him. He said to the man: "Go home and pray. I will also pray and wherever you go my prayers will be with you." At these words Savanio felt his pain leave him and he was cured again, this time for good!

"Go! Ride your bicycle!"

On getting out of bed on the morning of February 7th, 1947, Nicolas De Vincentiis, station-master at San Severo, had a bad fall which left him paralyzed.

His family ran to help him and put him onto a chair, then called the doctor. He could not diagnose the cause of the paralysis, and advised that he be taken to the Neurological Clinic in Rome. Here he underwent thorough examinations but nothing could be done to give him back the use of his legs. He could move a little by using crutches, but he was no longer in control of his body.

The unfortunate De Vincentiis went back home very demoralized and began a painful existence pulling himself around on crutches. He often fell, which aggravated his condition.

After a year of this he decided to go to San Giovanni Rotondo to see Padre Pio. The priest received him with kindness, comforted him and on taking his leave said: "Today is Friday. On Monday, take a ride on your bicycle and then make an appointment to be examined again in Rome." De Vincentiis did not understand. Who could ride a bicycle with legs that did not move? "Padre Pio is really odd!" he thought. "Does he realize what a bad state I am in? He seems to. Oh! Well, I'll do as he says. Who knows what might happen?"

On Monday De Vincentiis took out his bicycle and tried to get on, and it worked! "Is it possible I am cured?" he asked himself. Then, a few metres further on, he fell. Oh! Oh! Oh! What is happening? Someone put him back in the saddle and yet there was no one around! He put his feet on the pedals and this time everything went well. He wondered what had happened.

We read in the Gospel that St. Peter, one day, asked Jesus to help him walk on the water of the Lake of Genesareth during a wild storm. Jesus said to him: "Come!" Peter started out and then took fright and began to sink. He cried out: "Lord, save me!" The Lord took him by the hand and led him back into the boat saying: "Man of little faith! Why did you doubt?"

Had something like this happen to Nicolas? Probably! The fact is that on that memorable Monday he recovered the use of his limbs. He returned to Rome for further examinations and the professors confirmed he was completely cured.

Padre Pio confirms a cure in Switzerland

An engineer called Ferrazzini lived in the canton of Tessin, in Switzerland, with his twenty-one-year-old daughter who had been ill for a long time. Her name was Caterina Maria. One day she asked her father to take her to Padre Pio.

Ferrazzini granted her desire and set out with his daughter for San Giovanni Rotondo. It was a long journey and, when they finally arrived, they took rooms in a hotel. At this point something very unusual happened. As soon as she arrived in San Giovanni, Caterina's suffering ceased!

The next day she went to Padre Pio who heard her confession and gave her his blessing. A few days later Caterina and her father decided to bo back to Switzerland. The young girl continued to be in good health. On their return the doctor who had been treating her advised a checkup and Caterina went to the hospital for further examinations while her father went back to work.

One morning when taking out his car to go to his office, he saw Padre Pio near the garage. He took him to be his pastor but then quickly realized he was a Capuchin. Astonished he asked Padre Pio: "Father, what are you doing here?" "I have come to see how you are." Padre Pio replied. "Very well, Father," said Ferrazzini, "although, we are still a little concerned about Caterina. The results of her tests at the hospital have still to come through." "Don't worry," Padre Pio said, "everything will be all right." He gave his blessing and disappeared.

Ferrazzini was astounded, but encouraged by the priest's words. The results of Caterina's tests were, in fact, positive. Padre Pio through his mysterious gift of bilocation had come to confirm this cure which had taken place earlier in San Giovanni Rotondo and to bring the comfort of his presence.

Is Padre Pio mistaken?

Giuseppina Marchetti was living with her father in Bologna in July 1930. She was twenty-four and some years earlier had been is an accident resulting in a badly broken right arm. She had undergone an operation. Three years later, another operation proved unsuccessful and because of this she had to udergo a series of very painful treatments. After another examination the surgeon told her she would never recover the use of the arm because a bone-graft had not taken. Father and daughter were quite desolate.

What should they do? An idea came to mind. They knew Padre Pio and had confidence in him. Since modern science could not do anything, why not ask him to intercede with God for a cure?

At San Giovanni Rotondo Padre Pio greeted them with affection and encouraged them to trust in God and not to give up. Giuseppina would definitely be cured! He blessed them and took his leave.

The days went by and nothing happened. What was going on? Was Padre Pio mistaken? No, not at all. He had foreseen a long delay in the young girl's cure. Of course, the father and daughter knew nothing of this and went back to Bologna rather puzzled.

On the 17th of September 1930, Feast of the Stigmata of St. Francis, the Marchetti house was invaded by the scents of jonquils and roses and this lasted about fifteen minutes. It was the mysterious mark of Padre Pio who kept his promise.

Giuseppina's arm was healed. She realized very quickly that her arm was normal again and this was confirmed later by the X-Ray plates.

A cure during confession

One day, the playwright, Luigi Antonelli told a journalist of his extraordinary cure through the intervention of Padre Pio. His doctors had found a cancer covering the area between his ear and his shoulder and had spoken to him of an operation. He went to a surgeon and asked him: "How much time have I got left?" The surgeon replied: "With the operation six months and without it, three months." "All right," said Antonelli, "I'll have the operation. I can't turn down an extra three months of life!"

He would have undergone the operation had not one of his friends advised him to go to San Giovanni Rotondo and see Padre Pio. Perhaps the priest would ask the Lord to cure him without the operation. Antonelli reflected on this, then said: "Why not?" He set out for San Giovanni and when he arrived went immediately to the little church and attended Padre Pio's Mass. Afterwards, he went to confession.

What happened during this confession? Antonelli found it difficult to describe even though he was a man who had a way with words. During confession he had a long conversation with Padre Pio and the longer it went on, the more his soul was transported into a celestial state. At the same time he felt a kind of current circulating in his body, eradicating all traces of the cancer.

When he got off his knees, Antonelli felt in good health. His soul, as well as his body, had been cured. He took up all his activities again without ever experiencing again the slightest symptoms of cancer.

"He is the one I saw!"

Concetta Bellarmini was a pharmacist. In 1926 she contracted a blood infection and then, bronchial pneumonia. She was reduced to a wretched state. Her skin was yellow. As the doctors were unable to do anything for her, one of her relatives suggested that the sick woman should have recourse to Padre Pio, whom she had never met. Her children were against this as they did not believe in anything done by this friar from Gargano. But Concetta did not agree with them, and with great fervour invoked Padre Pio.

One day, when she was in bed, a Capuchin appeared in her room. Without touching her, he smiled and blessed her. She was not afraid of this apparition but was serene and peaceful afterwards. She asked him if his coming meant the grace of conversion for her children or her cure. The friar answered: "On Sunday morning you will return to good health." He then disappeared leaving behind an intense perfume which the servant also noticed.

When Sunday came, Concetta realized she had been cured and her skin had regained its normal colouring. She then wanted to go to San Giovanni Rotondo to meet Padre Pio and thank him. Her brother went with her on this journey. When they arrived at the monastery they asked which friar was Padre Pio. Someone pointed him out when he came through the crowd. Concetta Bellarmini recognized in him, the Capuchin who had appeared to her in her room at Lanciano and she cried out: "That's him! He is the one I saw!"

A new lease on life

Maria-Silvia, the daughter of Dr. Gaetano Benini who practiced medicine in Fontignano, was taken to a hospital in Perugia on October 15th, 1952. A final attempt was to be made to remove a cancer of the intestines. The operation, undertaken by distinguished surgeons, colleagues of Dr. Benini, was unsuccessful. He was resigned to taking his daughter home to die in her family. However, five days later she had a dream in which she saw the Child Jesus accompanied by Padre Pio.

The Child Jesus came to her and told her to let her parents know that they need not worry because Padre Pio had asked for and obtained her cure. The little girl, who was barely three years old, told all this to her mother and father when she awoke. She then got up and said she felt so well she wanted to go play with her friends. The parents were beside themselves with joy and could hardly believe what had happened, but the facts were there! Her father went off to San Giovanni Rotondo to thank Padre Pio. The priest welcomed him warmly and assured him that his little daughter was indeed cured. He also encouraged the doctor to be more attentive to his Christian duties.

Padre Pio and Giovannino

Gino was a docker in the port of Naples. He was active in the Communist Party and had great dreams for the future of the Marxist revolution. But as we say: "Don't count your chickens before they're hatched!"

One day he fell in love with a young girl called Francesca and he wanted to marry her. But she did not share his Marxist opinions. He was determined to marry her all the same and would try to find a way.

Alas! Francesca had an accident which affected her ability to have children. Still, he was determined to marry her because he loved her very much. A short time later they were indeed married and soon, Gino and Francesca were expecting a baby. Then the trouble began! Because of the consequences of her accident the doctors feared that she would not be able to give birth without endangering her own life. A choice had to be made between saving the baby or the mother. Francesca fell into a deep despondency. What should she do? Have an abortion? While she was thinking about this dilemma a Capuchin appeared unexpectedly in her room. He stood at the foot of her bed and said: "You must not do any such thing! You will have this child and it will be a boy and you will call him Giovanni."

Francesca had never seen Padre Pio but when she saw a photograph of him later, she recognized the Capuchin who had come to her room. Assured by his visit she was no longer in doubt. She would have the baby! Her parents were very much against her decision and could not believe it. She remained adamant and brought the baby into the world without any complications. Those who had warned her had to accept the evidence. The baby was baptized Giovanni. Gino, his father, confused by all this, had to face reality.

Padre Pio had opened a road to him somewhat different from that of the Marxist revolution. When he went with his wife to thank Padre Pio he promised that they would walk, with Giovanni, on the road of a fervent Christian life.

"She is better off in heaven!"

Father Alberto D'Apolito recounts that, one day, he received a telegram from a rich industrialist living in Piedmont. This man was a spiritual son of Padre Pio. He was asking Father Alberto to solicit Padre Pio's prayer for his wife, who was dying from an internal haemorrhage. He added that if his wife was cured he would give a large donation to the *Casa Sollievo della Sofferenza.*

Father Alberto passed on his friend's request to Padre Pio. Obviously moved, the priest assured him he would pray for the sick woman.

When, however, he heard there was a question of money being given if the cure happened, he changed his mind and said to Father Alberto: "We don't make deals with the Lord!" He added: "But, I will pray for the salvation of her soul." When he said this there were signs of great suffering on his face. At that very moment the industrialist's wife died, assisted by a priest.

A few days later, when Father Alberto told Padre Pio about her death, he cried out: "She is better off in heaven!"

"Woman! Why do you besiege me?"

A woman from San Giovanni watched her sick husband go from bad to worse and sink rapidly towards death. In great distress, she ran to the monastery to get Padre Pio to pray for his recovery. There was such a large crowd around the priest that she could not get near.

What should she do? Speak to him in confession? A long line of women were waiting for confession so she would be the last to have her turn. In deep thought she prayed interiorly that Padre Pio would help her husband who, at any moment, might die and leave her alone to bring up their children.

When she saw Padre Pio go the altar to celebrate Mass she dashed over there, but the crowd was just as big and she could not even see the priest! She tried going to the right, then the left but it was of no use. She could only go on praying, interiorly, filled with this anguish which wrenched her heart, because the inevitable could happen to her husband at any moment.

When Padre Pio finished Mass the poor woman managed to squeeze into the corridor he used to go to the monastery. There, again, she went on praying in her heart. Padre Pio came along and stopped by her saying: "Woman of little faith! Why do you besiege me and bombard me with your prayer? Do you think I'm deaf? You have already told me what you want, five times, from the right, the left, in front and behind! I have understood! I get the message! Go home! Everything is all right!" Full of joy, the woman thanked him and ran home as if she had wings on her feet. She arrived at her house, breathless, to find her husband in perfect health.

Padre Pio's healing scarf

Guiseppe Canaponi tells how, in the winter of 1954, he arrived at San Giovanni Rotondo, during a storm and pouring rain. He had to walk a good part of the road to the monastery and arrived cold, soaked to the skin, and he had lost his voice! As he was a close friend of Padre Pio he went straight up to his cell and found the priest in conversation with the Superior.

Canaponi greeted them both with his barely audible voice. Padre Pio seeing him in such a sorry state asked what had happened. He then touched him and said: "My poor friend, you are soaked through!" He turned to the Superior and asked: "Is there anything we can put around his shoulders to warm him?" The Superior did not have anything at hand. Then Padre Pio searched around his cell and finally found a large brown scarf hanging behind the door. "Lucky for you!" he said to Canaponi, "It is almost new. I have hardly worn it!" He then tied it round the man's neck. Canaponi felt a great warmth surge through his body and exclaimed: "I feel better already!" And in saying this he realized his voice had come back to normal. "You see!" said Padre Pio simply, "The warmth has done you good!"

"Do not move before Sunday!"

There was a young woman in San Giovanni Rotondo who often went to the monastery and to Padre Pio's Mass. She contracted a leg infection which kept her in bed for a long time. This meant she could not get to the monastery. She did everything she could to get well and to shorten her stay in bed, but the leg was healing very slowly. She grew impatient and one day got out of bed. She had a bad fall and her leg swelled up.

She had someone ask Padre Pio to pray for her because she was tired of waiting and wanted to go to Mass the following Sunday. Padre Pio replied: "It will be all right for Sunday. She will go to Mass but she must not move before then!" To the astonishment of her doctor, the young woman was completely healed and went to Mass the following Sunday.

"I will come with you."

An engineer from Rome, named Todini, who had come to visit Padre Pio, stayed with him long into the evening. As it was late, he wanted to get back to his hotel. When he opened the monastery door, he saw it was raining very heavily, and he had not brought an umbrella. What was to be done? It was a two-kilometer walk between the monastery and his hotel and in such heavy rain he would be soaked through and risk catching cold. He asked Padre Pio if there was any chance he could spend the night at the monastery. Padre Pio said it was impossible but told him to go back to his hotel without worrying about the rain as he would accompany him. Todini was not quite sure what this meant but set out all the same. A wonderful thing happened! The rain stopped suddenly and not one drop fell on Todini all the way from the monastery to the hotel. When he got there, the receptionist was very surprised he had walked back in such a downpour, assuming that he must be soaked through. Todini assured her that he was not wet and that, in fact, he was quite dry, and invited her to touch him to make sure! She did so and saw that he was indeed dry. She looked outside. The rain was still pouring down as it had been for over an hour. She could not understand: "What did you do to stay so dry?" she asked. The engineer replied: "Padre Pio said he would come with me and, as you can see, he kept the rain off me!" The woman exclaimed: "Padre Pio's company is certainly more effective than all the umbrellas in the world!"

"It is not yet time to go."

At the monastery in San Giovanni Rotondo lived a friar named Brother Léon de Tora. He had been sick for a long time with a painful illness causing him great suffering. Whenever Padre Pio returned to his cell after confessions, he never forgot to visit Brother Léon, inquire about his health and comfort him in his sufferings.

One day, as usual, Padre Pio went to see the sick Brother with some of his confrères, among them, Brother Daniel whom he had saved from certain death after much prayer and a great deal of suffering offered on his behalf. Padre Pio went over to the bed and asked Brother Léon how he was feeling. At the same time he unbuttoned the Brother's shirt and placed one of his mittens covering the stigmata on the sick man's neck.

Brother Léon felt he could not endure any more suffering and said to Padre Pio: "I want to die!" "Brother," said Padre Pio, "your train ticket is not yet ready!"

Brother Daniel followed Padre Pio to his cell and asked him: "What about me, Father, wasn't my ticket ready?" "Yes!" replied the priest. "Not only was your ticket ready, but the train as well! You will never know how much you cost me!"

"Don't say anything to anyone!"

Father Placido of San Marco in Lamis was a confrère of Padre Pio. They had been through the novitiate and studies together. In July, 1957 Father Placido fell seriously ill with cirrhosis of the liver and was taken to a hospital in San Severo.

One night, he saw Padre Pio standing near him, encouraging him and assuring him that he would recover. Padre Pio then went over to the window, put his hand on the glass and disappeared.

The next morning Father Placido experienced a great feeling of well-being throughout his body and got out of bed. He went to the window and saw the imprint of Padre Pio's hand on the glass. The news of this travelled fast around the hospital and people flocked to his room to see the imprint for themselves. Of course, the news spread outside the hospital too and people came in off the streets, so there was a lot of coming and going; this upset the hospital's routine. The hospital authorities had to intervene. Other people just laughed at such a ridiculous happening but Father Placido kept on insisting that Padre Pio had come and left the imprint of his hand on the window. They tried to clean off the imprint but it would not wash away and remained there for some time.

Father Alberto D'Apolito, who was in San Severo at the time, visited the hospital and saw this phenomenon for himself. He wanted to be sure that Padre Pio had, in fact, come to the hospital, so, on his next visit to San Giovanni, he asked him. Padre Pio replied: "Yes, I went to the hospital but don't say anything to anyone!"

7

APPEALS FROM BEYOND THE GRAVE

The aim of Christian life is to be with God forever. To reach this goal, Christians must prepare themselves in this world, so that they may be worthy to be with Him.

Many do not think of this preparation and others do not get time as their life is cut off when they least expect it. This means that, after death, some have more preparation to do before reaching the Vision of God.

It would seem that God sometimes allows certain souls to ask for help from those still on earth. Padre Pio received many such requests from these "beggars" beyond the grave, although he did not often speak about this. He has, however, left an impressive account including the following occurrences.

Four deceased friars visit the monastery

Padre Pio told this story in San Giovanni one evening in February 1922 to the *"fratini"*, young boys educated by the Capuchins.

"Listen and I will tell you what happened to me a few days ago. I came down one night, to warm myself at the fireplace in the community room and was surprised to find four friars there sitting beside the fire in silence and with their cowls pulled down. I greeted them as we usually do with: 'Praised be Jesus Christ!' but no one responded. Astonished, I looked at them closely to find out who they were but I did not recognize any of them. I stood there for several minutes watching them and it seemed to me they were in some kind of pain. I greeted them again, but there was no response.

I then went off to find out if we had some visiting friars staying with us. Father Superior said to me: 'Padre Pio, who would venture up here in such terrible weather?' I said to him: 'But Father Guardian, downstairs around our fire, there are four Capuchins sitting on the benches, with their cowls pulled down, warming themselves. I greeted them but they did not answer and I did not recognize them when I looked closely. I don't know who they are!'

Father Guardian exclaimed: 'Is it possible that some visiting Brothers have arrived without anyone letting me know? Let's go and see!'

When we got there we did not find anyone by the fire! I understood then, that they must have been dead religious who were undergoing their Purgatory here, where they had offended God. I spent the whole night before the Blessed Sacrament, praying for their deliverance."

The old man who was burned alive

Padre Pio told the following story one afternoon in May 1922 to Msgr. Alberto Costa, Bishop of Melfi.

"We were in the middle of World War II and the monastery at San Giovanni Rotondo, like all other monasteries at the time, was rather empty. The friars had been called up to the army. The Seraphic College was moved to the monastery and Father Paolino da Casacalenda and I were in charge. One winter afternoon, Assunta di Tommaso, Father Paolino's sister, arrived at the monastery. She had come to visit her brother for a few days. There was thick snow everywhere. Father Paolina advised his sister to make her way to the village before nightfall and stay with Rachelina Russo, a benefactor of the monastery.

Assunta refused to go out alone in such deep snow, afraid she might meet with a stray and hungry wolf or be attacked by some marauder. Father Paolino reminded her that the rules of Enclosure did not allow women to enter the cloister. What was to be done? 'Make up a bed here in this room just for tonight,' Assunta said, 'and I will go to Rachelina tomorrow.' 'Good!' said Father Paolino. 'If you are happy to spend the night here, I will have a bed made up for you and you can sleep here in peace.'

He called some of the boys to make up a camp bed and light a fire in the room. After supper, when the boys were in bed, Father Paolino and I went down to see Assunta. Some time later, Father Paolina said to his sister: 'I am going to say a Rosary in the church. You can stay and chat with Padre Pio.'

She said she would rather go with him, so they went off together.

On leaving, they closed the door and I sat alone by the fire. I was praying, with my eyes half-closed, when the door opened and an old man came in dressed in the kind of cloak the San Giovanni Rotondo peasants wore. He sat down beside me. I looked at him and wondered how he had got into the monastery at this hour. 'Who are you and what do you want?' I asked him. 'Padre Pio,' he replied. 'I am Pietro Di Moro, son of the late Nicolas, nicknamed, Precoco. I died in this monastery on the 18th of September 1908, in cell No. 4, when there used to be a shelter for beggars here. One night I fell asleep in bed smoking a cigarette. I set fire to the mattress and I was suffocated and burned to death. I am still in Purgatory and I need one Mass for my deliverance. The Lord has allowed me to ask your help.' I told him to be at peace and that I would say a Mass the next day, for his deliverance.

I got up and walked him to the monastery door, to let him out. I saw that the door was locked and barred. I opened it and the old man left. The moon was shining brightly on the snow-covered square. It was almost as clear as day. When I could not see the old man anymore. I felt a kind of fear, closed the door, and went back to the room, trembling.

Father Paolino and his sister returned after reciting the Rosary. When they saw how pale and ashen I was they thought I was feeling sick. Having said goodnight to his sister Father Paolino walked me to my cell. I did not say a word about the dead man.

A few days after Assunta left, Father Paolino wanted to know what had happened the night I did not feel well. I told him in great detail of my encounter with this apparition from beyond the grave, and added: 'I couldn't say in front of your sister that the dead had visited me, because she would not have slept in that room!' "

Father Paolino wanted to check out what the beggar had told Padre Pio. He went to the City Hall, where the registers confirmed everything the beggar had told Padre Pio.

The novice in the unlit church

Another incident concerned the apparition of a novice. Padre Pio was praying one night in the sanctuary when he heard a noise near the altar. Thinking that someone had come into the church with evil intent, he called out: "Who's there?" There was no response.

He went back to his prayer, thinking that it had been the wind, but he heard the noise again. Padre Pio went over to the choir grill and looked towards the high altar. There he saw a young novice cleaning. "What are you doing over there?" Padre Pio asked. "I'm cleaning." replied the novice. "But," asked Padre Pio, "how can you do that in the dark?" The young man replied: "I am a Capuchin novice doing my Purgatory here and I need help." Then, he disappeared!

Next day, Padre Pio came to his aid by celebrating Mass for him.

All his illnesses were over!

Padre Pio related the following to Father Bernardino d'Apicella. On the 29th of December 1936, Father Giacinto di Sant'Elia in Pianisi came from Foggia to San Giovanni Rotondo to ask prayers for the dying Father Giuseppantonio of San Marco in Lamis.

Padre Pio assured him he would pray for the dying man. He spent that day going about his priestly duties and the next day, the 30th of December, as well. That night he went to his cell and was preparing for bed when he saw Father Giuseppantonio standing in front of him. Surprised, Padre Pio asked him: "How did you get here? I was told you are very seriously ill, and yet, here you are!" Father Giuseppantonio made a sign indicating that he was dead and also to let him know that all his illnesses were over!

A friend visits from beyond the grave

On March 7th, 1988, I was passing by Trevi, the home of the Marchioness Giovanna Boschi of whom I spoke earlier. I stopped by to find out about an apparition the Marchioness had had of her friend, Marguerite Hamilton, three days after her death. She gave me the following details.

Marguerite had confided to her friend that, during her last confession with Padre Pio, he had assured her he would be with her at the moment of her death and bless her three times.

One day, in 1974, Marguerite said to the Marchioness: "Padre Pio often appears in dreams to other people, but not to me!" However, on April 29th, 1974, she told her friend, Giovanna: "Tonight, Padre Pio appeared to me in a dream, and blessed me three times. The hour of my death is at hand."

The Marchioness told her it was only a dream and that she should not take it so seriously. The two friends made a pact that whoever died first should, God willing, come back and tell the other about her state in the next world. That same afternoon the Marchioness went to see Marguerite, who had calmed down a bit, so that they could talk together again of the dream and she could give her some comfort. While they were talking Marguerite went white and collapsed, and died of a stroke. Giovanna was overcome with emotion and grief.

Three days after the funeral, while the Marchioness was resting on her bed, saying the Rosary, she saw Marguerite sitting in her husband Fernando's armchair! She thought this must be an hallucination and, rubbing her eyes, looked again and again. Her friend was still there and a light shone from her. Finally, the Marchioness took her courage in both hands and asked if she was her friend Marguerite. "Yes!" replied the woman in the armchair. It was indeed Marguerite who had come back to tell her that Padre Pio had assisted her in her last moments and that she was safe and happy. She then disappeared.

8

PADRE PIO'S FAMILIARITY
WITH HIS GUARDIAN ANGEL

For most of us, our guardian angel is a great unknown. For Padre Pio, on the contrary, he was well-known and worked with him on his sanctification and his priestly ministry. Between them there was a kind of bond. You could almost say they lived together.

The very exceptional, spiritual life of Padre Pio necessitated exceptional assistance on the part of his guardian angel. Again, his priestly ministry, replete with so many charisms, demanded a great deal of this help, in a variety of ways, such as: being a messenger to people in touch with Padre Pio; translating foreign languages, etc... Here are some glimpses of this familiarity which existed between Padre Pio and his guardian angel.

Padre Pio reproaches his guardian angel

Once, Padre Pio was violently attacked by the devil and his cohort, whom he called "cossacks". The struggle was so intense that Padre Pio, at one point, thought he had lost, so he called out his guardian angel for help. But the angel did not come and he had to fight on alone. As usual, though, Padre Pio threw himself completely into the struggle and prayed with greater intensity than ever. In the end he came out of it victorious but exhausted.

The angel appeared. Padre Pio was really angry with him and reproached him for not coming when he called out so urgently for his help. Then, as if he wanted to "punish" the angel, he turned away without even looking at him. The angel followed him looking dejected and nearly in tears!

Eventually, when they were reconciled the angel explained it was not negligence that had kept him away, but God had wanted Padre Pio to come through this battle unaided.

Padre Pio speaks English without ever learning it!

Angelina Sorritelli, daughter of an Italian emigrant to the United States was born in America and spoke only English. Her father, Tommaso, took her to San Giovanni Rotondo because he wanted Padre Pio to hear her confession and give her First Communion.

At this time, Maria Pyle, an American convert, was living in a house near the monastery and she helped in Padre Pio's work. As soon as she heard the girl had arrived, she offered her services as interpreter to Angelina. She even went to Padre Pio and also offered him her services in this situation. Padre Pio thanked her but said he would deal with

Angelina directly. Amazed, Miss Pyle withdrew and Padre Pio heard the little girl's confession.

When it was over, Miss Pyle asked the child: "Did you understand what Padre Pio said?" "Yes," she said. "And he understood you?" she asked. "Yes," the girl answered again. "And what did he speak, English?" Miss Pyle went on. "Yes," said the girl, "he spoke in English."

Padre Pio speaks German

Professor Bruno Rabajotti tells that, one day, he was in Padre Pio's cell, reciting the Rosary with him.

When they had finished, someone brought in a German visitor, a tall, thin man with short white hair. He began to thank Padre Pio, in German, for the wonderful things that had happened to his daughter.

The conversation continued for a while with questions and answers between the two men. Rabajotti could hardly believe his ears. Padre Pio was speaking German and looked over at him, from time to time, with a twinkle in his eye! Eventually, Padre Pio said to him: "You seem surprised to hear me speak and understand a language I don't know. I am not the only one who can do that. Why don't you try?" "But I don't know any German, Father!" "Neither do I," the priest said, "but it is easy. All you have to do is begin speaking. This man, who came here, a year ago, will tell you his story. Differences of language and barriers between souls disappear, when we speak the only language that really matters, that of the spirit."

Professor Rabajotti did as Padre Pio told him, and to his utter amazement he was able to hold a conversation with the man, in German! During this time, Padre Pio stood with his arms crossed watching, and absolutely delighted.

The professor went on to say: "Although we spoke in German I thought I was speaking Italian. It was so easy and so beautiful. Before leaving we embraced."

An unusual mail carrier

Cleonice Morcaldi, a woman from San Giovanni Rotondo, told us a strange story. During World War II, one of her nephews was taken prisoner. For over a year the family had no news of him. They suspected the worst. One day, Cleonice went to Padre Pio, threw herself at his feet and begged him to tell her at least whether her nephew was alive or dead!

The priest reassured her and said: "Get up and go in peace." Even if his words gave her hope, she was still full of doubts. The days passed and no news came. Her anxiety increased all the more. Finally, she decided to try out something, even if it seemed a bit foolish! Sustained by her great faith she went back to Padre Pio and said to him: "Let's try this. I will write a letter to my nephew, but I can only put his name on the envelope, because I don't know where he is. It's up to you and your guardian angel to see that he gets it!" Padre Pio said nothing, but Cleonice thought to herself, silence means consent. Her hope was renewed.

That night, she wrote the letter before going to sleep and put it on the bedside table. The next morning, her surprise was mixed with fear when she noticed the letter had disappeared. She ran to Padre Pio who said to her: "Thank the Blessed Virgin!"

Fifteen days later, she received a reply to her letter, and in it she read the good news that Giovannino was alive. He enclosed his address, saying he would see her again soon.

A spiritual daughter makes herself heard

When Padre Pio was forbidden to write to his spiritual sons and daughters, some asked him: "Father, what are we going to do since you cannot write to us?" He replied: "Send your guardian angel instead!"

One of his spiritual daughters, who actively helped in Padre Pio's work and enterprises, was fully aware that Padre Pio was forbidden to keep in touch with the outside world. In spite of that, she insisted on seeing Padre Pio, because she urgently needed to speak with him for the good of her soul. Padre Pio replied that, because he was anxious to obey the orders he had received, he could not come to the parlour.

This woman, who was more concerned about her personal needs than about Padre Pio's situation, was very annoyed and complained of being treated in this way, especially after all she had done for the priest and the monastery. Back home, she told her guardian angel to let Padre Pio know she would not be at Mass or Communion the next day.

Evidently, the guardian angel had carried out her order because, that very evening, Padre Pio replied saying: "Tell Rachelina not to go to Communion tomorrow!"

The next day, Rachelina, nevertheless, went to the monastery to work, as usual, with her colleague, Lucietta Fiorentino. While she was working Padre Pio appeared and said to her: "Bravo! Your guardian angel is your messenger. At your imperious command he brought me all your rage!" He then turned to Lucietta and said: "Do you know, Lucietta, what this woman has done? Out of anger, she decided she would not go to Mass or Holy Communion, then she arrogantly commanded her guardian angel to let me know!"

Rachelina was greatly embarrassed and asked: "Father, did my guardian angel really go and tell you everything?" "Of course he did," Padre Pio answered. "He is not disobedient like you!"

Padre Pio's considerate guardian angel!

At one time, Padre Pio was ill and had to keep to his bed. Father Paolino da Casacalenda, his Superior, often came to see him. One night he said to him: "Father, if you need me during the night, send your guardian angel." Padre Pio said he would certainly do so.

Father Paolino went to bed. Around midnight his bed was violently shaken. Half awake in his slumber, he knew that Padre Pio's guardian angel had come for him but he was so overcome by fatigue and drowsiness that he fell back into a deep sleep.

The next morning he told Padre Pio what had happened and how mortified he felt about not coming to him. He suggested that, next time, the guardian angel should shake the bed a little harder. That night the guardian angel came and shook the bed very strongly, but again, the priest could not wake up completely and fell back asleep.

Feeling more and more humiliated by all this he went to Padre Pio and said he should ask his guardian angel to treat him less delicately, otherwise he would never wake up. The angel must really shake the bed in such a way that he would be up and running to Padre Pio.

On the third night, the guardian angel came and shook the bed so violently that the priest leapt out and ran to ask what Padre Pio wanted. The priest said to him: "I am in a sweat! Help me change my clothes, please, as I cannot do it myself."

9

ON FIRST NAME TERMS WITH
THE DEVIL, BARBABLU!

A priest like Padre Pio, destined by the Lord to do great things for the Glory of God and the salvation of souls, could not escape the fierce opposition of the sworn enemy of God and man, the devil. Padre Pio nicknamed him, *Barbablu* (Bluebeard). Padre Pio had to confront him from his very first steps on the road to sanctity and kept up a continual and particularly terrifying battle with him.

This hard-fought battle cost him great sacrifices and had severe physical consequences, but he always won! Here are some encounters in this war between Padre Pio and Satan.

A ferocious dog

The following episode was told by Padre Pio himself in a letter written to Father Agostino, his spiritual director.

"It happened when I was studying philosophy at Sant'Elia in Pianisi. I had the second last cell in the corridor leading to the church, at about the height of the statue of the Immaculate Conception over the high altar.

"One night, after Matins, I had opened the door and the window because the heat was unbearable. Suddenly I heard noises apparently coming from the cell next door and wondered what Fra Atanasio could be doing at that hour. Thinking he was keeping a prayer vigil I began to recite the Rosary. We had challenged each other to see who could pray the most and I did not want to be left behind! But the noises continued and grew louder and I wanted to call my confrère. There was a strong smell of sulphur. I leaned out the window to call him. (Our windows were so close we could easily pass something from one to the other.) 'Fra Atanasio! Fra Atanasio!' I called, without raising my voice too much. As there was no response I came away from the window, but to my horror, I saw a huge dog, smoke pouring from its jaws, come through the door. I fell back on my bed and heard it say: 'He is the one! He is the one!' Still lying there, I watched this horrible beast leap onto the roof opposite and disappear."

The next day, Fra Pio learned that Fra Atanasio had not been in his cell that night because he was away from the monastery. He then tried to find out who owned this animal from the local people, but no one could tell him. He was then convinced that the devil had come in the guise of this beast and that he would continue to come day and night in one form or another.

During these apparitions, the devil nearly always took forms that were obscene, bestial or monstrous. At times he would take angelic forms and even appeared in the form of St. Francis, the Blessed Virgin and Christ Himself!

Padre Pio wrote: "Barbablu does not want to admit defeat! He has taken every imaginable form. For several days he visited me with his helpers, armed with sticks and iron instruments and, what is worse, looking ugly and horrible. The last night was the worst. This "cossack" kept striking me, from about ten o'clock at night, when I usually go to bed, until five o'clock in the morning. He made diabolical suggestions to me, for example, thoughts of despair and giving up trust in God. I thought this must be the last night of my life or that I would go off my head. But, praised be to Jesus, nothing like this happened. However, at five o'clock in the morning, when the "cossack" left, a chill spread all over my body and I began to shake like a reed in the wind. This lasted two hours and I spat up blood."

A bogus confessor

Padre Pio was ill one day in the monastery at Venafro. Suddenly the door opened and someone came in who looked like Padre Pio's confessor, Father Agostino da San Marco in Lamis. This was the devil. He came over to Padre Pio and said he had come to hear his confession. Padre Pio looked at him closely and saw that he did, indeed, look like Father Agostino, but he was not completely convinced, as he found something strange about his face.

Moreover, he experienced the nausea he felt whenever the devil was present. To make sure that it was Father Agostino, he exclaimed: "Say, 'Jesus

Christ forever!' " At that moment, the false Father Agostino yelled: "No!" and immediately disappeared.

From disbelief to terror

Padre Pio had to deal with the devil over a long period of time and he became used to his apparitions, his harassments and the struggles out of which the priest always emerged victorious, even if, physically, he was in bad shape.

After many months in his home village of Pietrelcina, in the Province of Benevent, where he was trying to recover his health, which had been so mysteriously assailed, he received orders to go to the monastery of Sant'Anna in Foggia.

With his arrival, the monastery lost its customary peace because the devil followed Padre Pio to his new home. Every night, at the same time, strange noises could be heard, culminating in a loud explosion. Padre Pio was tempted in every way, attacked, mistreated, dragged from one place to another in an indescribable uproar. When the devil saw he could not win he released him with an infernal noise.

Padre Pio's confrères were afraid and upset by all this. They hoped it would end soon. On the contrary, it continued to the great consternation of everyone.

One day, Mgr. Andrea D'Agostino, Bishop of Ariano Irpino, arrived at the monastery and asked for hospitality.

In the course of conversation mention was made of the terrible noises that came from Padre Pio's cell when he was fighting the devil. The bishop listened, but made light of it, saying that, in his opinion, this was utter nonsense and should not be believed. However, that very night he was forced to change his mind! The bishop was so terrified he wanted to leave the monastery right away, but it was two in the morning and there were no means of transportation. He had to stay, but he insisted that a friar remain in the room with him throughout the rest of the night! The next morning he left very quickly and with very different ideas from those he had had the night before! Seeing, or rather hearing, is believing!

"Stay awhile!"

At the monastery of Sant'Anna in Foggia, Padre Pio had a confrère called Fra Francesco de Torremaggiore. He often went to Padre Pio's cell in the evening to keep him company. Padre Pio appreciated this very much because, as long as Fra Francesco was there, the "cossacks" did not come. One night, as usual, Fra Francesco went up to Padre Pio's cell for a chat. However, on that night he was very tired and kept dropping off to sleep. He stood up, eventually, and made as if to leave, but Padre Pio said to him: "Stay awhile, because, if you don't, they (the "cossacks") will come." So Fra Francesco stayed a bit longer although he was very drowsy. Finally, he said he really had to go, because he could not stay awake any longer. "Go, Brother, go!" said Padre Pio.

Fra Francesco had hardly taken ten steps when he heard the most terrible noise coming from Padre Pio's cell. He went straight back and found him completely exhausted and soaked in sweat, from the struggle he had with the demons. They had come as usual to attack Padre Pio, taking advantage of Fra Francesco's departure.

"You will not hear it again."

All this noise, night after night, eventually tried the patience of the friars beyond endurance, especially one of them, who although he was kind and understanding, was always on edge and on the verge of a nervous breakdown. One evening, when he was in the refectory with the others, the terrible noises started again, above his head, where Padre Pio's room was located. In a fit of anger, he yelled: "Is this never going to end?"

This was reported to Padre Pio who said in a resigned way: "They must not hear this again." He prayed to the Lord for this intention and, from that time on, the friars heard no further noise.

This did not mean, however, that the devil ceased to torment Padre Pio. On the contrary, the priest had to carry this terrible cross alone.

Interference with the mail

When Padre Pio was living in Pietrelcina for the good of his health, he kept up a correspondence with his spiritual director, Father Agostino. But he was, at the same time, under the immediate direction of the archpriest, Dom Salvatore Pannullo, who was quick to realize that he was dealing with a special penitent. He took every precaution to make sure his people would not be misled by this extraordinary man.

As one of these precautions, he had agreed with Padre Pio that each letter sent by Father Agostino should be shown to him first. One day, Padre Pio received a letter and brought it to Dom Salvatore. When he opened it, he found a blank sheet of paper inside.

He said to Padre Pio: "Father Agostino must have made a mistake and put this blank paper in the envelope instead of a letter." "Father Agostino did not make a mistake," Padre Pio said. "There is writing on it, but Barbablu has made it illegible. Dom Salvatore exclaimed: "So *you* know what is written there?" "Yes, I know," said Padre Pio, and repeated all that Father Agostino had written.

Dom Salvatore was taken aback by this. To check the truth of the matter he wrote, with haste, to Father Agostino to see if he had really written what Padre Pio had said. Father Agostino confirmed this, word for word!

Another time, a letter arrived, but, in the middle of the sheet of paper was a large stain, shaped like a funnel, making it impossible to read the writing. This time, Dom Salvatore took holy water and sprinkled it on the stain which disappeared, so that he was able to read the letter without difficulty.

An exorcism in the sacristy

One Sunday afternoon in May 1922, some people brought a possessed woman to the sacristy of the little monastery church at San Giovanni Rotondo.

After the evening service of the Benediction of the Blessed Sacrament, Padre Pio went to the sacristy and was confronted with the unfortunate woman. She began yelling, swearing and blaspheming, while she was shaking with convulsions.

Padre Pio, calm and resolute, began the rite of Exorcism. But still, she continued to yell and lash about. The priest went through the rite undisturbed. Suddenly, the demon fled! The woman found her peace and tranquillity again, and behaved as if nothing had happened.

Padre Pio pays dearly

In 1964, a young girl was brought from a village near Bergamo to the Capuchin monastery at San Severo. She was possessed, and her friends took her there to see Father Placido de San Marco in Lamis, renowned for his sanctity. They wanted him to free her from the demon. When the girl saw Father Placido, she began to yell curses and blasphemies and even tried to attack him. After some deliberation the friars suggested to Father Placido that he send the possessed girl to Padre Pio at San Giovanni Rotondo.

She reacted in exactly the same way with Padre Pio. At that time Padre Pio did not have the physical strength to deal with such an exorcism so he only blessed her.

A few days later, other priests, authorized by the Archbishop of Manfredonia, tried to exorcise the unfortunate girl and drive out the demon. The fiend laughed at them for trying to exorcise him after they had been eating and drinking instead of praying and fasting! This plunged Padre Pio into great sadness and reflection.

During that night, he was furiously attacked by the devil who kicked him violently on his spine. He had a bad fall, cutting his eyebrow and causing his face to swell up. As he fell, he cried out and his confrères came running and found him in this state. Padre Pio told them he had fallen. He was unable to leave his cell next morning to celebrate Mass.

Meanwhile, the demon in the possessed girl was yelling that Padre Pio could not come down for Mass because he, the devil, had fixed him up! In fact, the Father Superior had to announce that Padre Pio would not be coming down that day. The large crowd who had gathered at the usual Mass time was greatly disturbed and somewhat disillusioned when they heard all this.

That same morning, the Superior of the monastery in San Severo, Father Alberto D'Apolito, arrived at San Giovanni Rotondo where he was told about all that had happened. He asked Padre Pio to confirm what the demon had said. He just said: "It is possible!" Grieved, Father Alberto then told Padre Pio how sorry he was to have sent the possessed girl to him. "You sent me a fine gift, didn't you?" Padre Pio said.

However, the struggle between Padre Pio and the devil for this young girl was not over. The priest prayed, did penance, and then, barely recovered from his ordeal, went down to celebrate Mass.

This time, when she saw him, the possessed girl shrieked and fainted. The demon left her. She was now calm and at peace, and attended Padre Pio's Mass before going home, completely cured. As usual, Padre Pio won this battle with the devil but he had to pay dearly!

Padre Pio gives "Barbablu" a kick

In 1946, a woman from Bottegone began to experience persistent physical ailments. She had sudden pains in her knees, her legs or in other parts of the body, as well as abdominal swelling. This generally happened when she was praying or went to church. The doctors she consulted could offer no remedy.

She spoke of this to a priest from Pistoia who, after giving her a blessing, advised her to see Padre Pio. As soon as she could, she went to San Giovanni Rotondo and took her turn for confession, thinking she could speak to him there about her concerns. As soon as Padre Pio appeared for confessions her whole body swelled up and she began to yell and scream. Padre Pio, who recognized the presence of "Barbablu" in the woman, went up to her and kicked her, saying in a commanding voice: "Go! Satan!" The woman fainted and, when she recovered, realized she had been delivered from the devil.

While two policemen escorted her through the crowd Padre Pio blessed her and said: "Go, thank our Heavenly Mother who has cured you!"

"Barbablu" takes over Padre Pio's confessional

Father Benedetto from San Marco in Lamis was Padre Pio's Provincial Superior and spiritual director. One day he had to question Padre Pio on his actions, and thus unveiled a nasty trick of "Barbablu". This is what happened.

A young girl from Cerignola had got it into her head that she was damned. She could not find a minute's peace because of this. Her mother decided to take her to Padre Pio so that he could free her from this torture.

They went to San Giovanni Rotondo and the girl went to Padre Pio for confession. She heard, from behind the grill, what she presumed to be his voice, but it was, in fact, the demon imitating Padre Pio's voice to perfection! He said to her: "Yes, indeed you are damned!"

One can imagine the turmoil this girl experienced and the despair she felt! She came out of the confessional, more anguished than before, and told everyone: "I am damned! Padre Pio himself told me!"

The incident came to the notice of Father Benedetto, who considered it his duty to confront Padre Pio: "Oh! my son!" he said, "What have you done? That poor girl will never find peace again! You must understand that, even if the Lord reveals to you something like this, you are not necessarily authorized to tell the unfortunate person concerned."

Padre Pio was thunderstruck, and told him he would never dream of saying such a thing to anyone. It was clear that "Barbablu" had tortured this girl in order to stir things up and cause trouble.

Padre Pio begged Father Benedetto to find the girl and bring her back.

She returned and went to Padre Pio for confession and afterwards she was at peace again.

10

A MODEL OF A SOLDIER

When Padre Pio reached conscription age, he was called up for military service just like other young men. This happened in November 1915. His time in the army was short, because his state of health did not allow him to fully take part in military life. He was no more than a sampling of a soldier.

This chapter in his career, however, gave him some idea of life in the barracks. He has given us the following delightful accounts of this experience. He said at one point: "I got more out of this ordeal than from any spiritual retreat I have ever made!"

Padre Pio risks a court martial

Padre Pio was called up as Francesco Forgione, serial number: 2094/25, on the 6th of November 1915. He went to the Military District of Benevent and joined the 10th Medical Corps of Naples. He stayed there only until the 10th of December that year, because he had constant attacks of fever. He was discharged for a year. When the year was over he went back to Naples and lasted only fifteen days. He was again sent home, this time for six months. On his discharge papers the military authorities had written: "When this leave is over, await further orders."

The months went by and the military authorities in Naples expected Padre Pio to return. They had obviously forgotten what they had written on his papers. As he did not return they gave orders to the police in Pietrelcina, his home village, and in San Giovanni Rotondo, his monastery at the time, to find Private Francesco Forgione. This, of course, was Padre Pio's name to the authorities. The police searched everywhere but could not find Francesco Forgione. By chance, they discovered that the soldier and Padre Pio were one and the same person so Padre Pio, now aware that they were looking for him, went back to Naples.

The military authorities looked on his absence as desertion and punishable by Court Martial. He showed them his leave papers and told them that the orders he awaited never came through! They accepted his explanation and believed his good intentions and so he escaped a trial in the Military Courts.

Private Forgione finds a safe place for his possessions

Contrary to what one would think, Private Forgione enjoyed military service. He was so thin that the uniform hung on him! With his sense of humour he described himself like this: "My mother made me a man, St. Francis made me a woman, (referring to his long, religious habit), and the government has made me a clown!''

When he realized that petty theft was the order of the day in the barracks and that tricks were played on the soldiers by the soldiers, he tried to find a way of avoiding all this. Finally, he decided he would *wear* everything he owned! He was so thin, and the uniform so big, that he could do this without any difficulty!

One day, he was called for a medical examination and asked to undress. Private Forgione calmly began to take off all he was wearing. First came one jacket, then another, a pair of trousers, then a second pair, a shirt and then another, and so on! When the Major saw all the soldier was wearing, he said: ''Private Forgione, you are not wearing a set of clothes but a store!''

Padre Pio takes a cab in Naples

Shortly after Padre Pio arrived in Naples, he wrote to his father, Orazio, to send him some ''goodies'' from his village of Pietrelcina.

Uncle Orazio, as he was called, filled a basket with olive oil, goat's cheese and juicy grapes and set off for Naples. The people of his village usually stayed at a boarding house run by Carolina del Maestro, who was also born in Pietrelcina.

Orazio called a taxi to take him to the Pension of Carolina. The driver pretended to know where he was going, but took his client through all the streets of Naples until Orazio began to realize that the man had no idea where he was going! He was able to give the driver directions and eventually they arrived at the boarding house. Orazio was annoyed with the driver for giving him the runaround, so, when he paid, he gave the man only 50¢ instead of the 75¢ he had demanded. There was nothing the driver could do about it. No one fooled around with Orazio Forgione!

At Carolina's place, he asked about his son. She told him he would be coming soon.

A few minutes later Padre Pio arrived in a cab. Orazio, seeing his son drive up in a cab, asked: "What can be left of the 75¢ you got for saying Mass, if you gave 50¢ to the cabdriver and 25¢ to the sacristan?" Padre Pio reassured him by saying that he was able to afford this because he was celebrating Mass in a private chapel and was given 15 liras!

Father and son enjoyed the good food from the village and then went for a walk along the Corso Umberto also known as *Rettifilo* (Straight Road). When the time came to part, Orazio was overcome by emotion and began to cry. Padre Pio consoled him by saying that he would not be staying in the army for long.

In fact on November 5th, 1917, he was sent on leave to Pietrelcina and then to San Giovanni. On the 17th of March 1918, he was discharged from the army. So ended this brief period of conscription for Private Francesco Forgione!

With a pass and one *lira* in his pocket

In December 1916, Padre Pio got a sickleave and went to Pietrelcina. He had to take the train from

Naples to Benevent and then take a bus to his village. The train fare was paid by the army and he was given one lira to cover the rest, that is, his bus ticket and anything else.

When he left the military hospital he walked through Naples enjoying the people of the city with their special way of talking and behaving. On one of the squares he came across a small market that sold everything. Padre Pio thought it would be a nice gesture to bring a little souvenir to his nephews but how could he manage to do this with one lira in his pocket? A trader came up to him, offering to sell little paper umbrellas. He said they were worth one lira each, but came down to 50¢ and then 40¢! Padre Pio made some calculations and said to himself: "If I spend my money on these little umbrellas, there will be nothing left!" He left the seller, high and dry, and went off to Garibaldi Station.

When his ticket was validated, he went to the train and, on the way, met another man selling paper umbrellas. This one called out to him in dialect: "Corporal! Corporal! Buy some of these lovely little umbrellas and give them as souvenirs to your children!" Padre Pio paid no attention, but when the man insisted, he said: "Listen! I don't want them and I have no need of them. In any case, you are not honest. In the market, they sell for 50¢ and you want 1.50L." The vendor tried again: "Corporal! I have three children. Help me make a little money. Please, please take the umbrellas as souvenirs for your children!" Padre Pio said: "Will you give them to me for 50¢?" The train had started to move, so Padre Pio jumped on and leaned out the window. He was moved with compassion for this poor man and threw

50¢ at him saying: "Here! Take it all and God bless you!" The man saluted and thanked him and having picked up his 50¢ went off very happy, while Padre Pio started on his journey to Benevent.

He arrived late at night and tried to find a corner where he could pass the long hours, because his bus was due to leave only at five o'clock in the morning. He could not find a place anywhere. The waiting room and the bar were full of soldiers. He tried walking up and down to keep himself warm, but became tired and went back to the waiting room. It was a case of standing room only, but at least he was sheltered from the cold. He spent a few hours like this.

He would have liked to go the bar for some coffee to warm up his insides. How could he do this? Not only were all the tables occupied but he had only 50¢ in his pocket. Presently he noticed two empty tables and sidled over to one of them, trying not to be noticed. One officer and two non-commissioned officers sat down at the other table. The waiter came and took their order and then moved to Padre Pio's table. There was nothing to do but order a cup of coffee! While waiting, he realized that his money was running out and that he might not be able to finish his journey. When the coffee arrived, he drank it very slowly so that he would be able to stay at the table until the bus for Pietrelcina arrived. When it came, Padre Pio went to the counter to pay for his coffee. The waiter told him: "Everything has been arranged! Your coffee is paid for!" How strange!

In the bus, Padre Pio went to the back so that he could explain to the conductor, without being noticed too much by the other passengers, that he did not have enough money for his fare but he would pay it in full on arriving at the village. The fare cost 1.80L! Just before the bus left, a distinguished gentleman got on and sat down beside Padre Pio. He had a little case and brought out a thermos and a glass, which he filled with hot coffee and gave to Padre Pio, while he drank from the thermos cup. When the conductor came for the tickets he said to Private Forgione: "Soldier! your ticket has been paid for!" Yet again, Padre Pio was taken by surprise and asked: "But who paid for me?" He thought it must have been the gentleman who sat down beside him. When he arrived at his destination he looked around to thank his benefactor but he had suddenly disappeared!

11

PADRE PIO'S SENSE OF HUMOUR

Carlo Campanini, one of Padre Pio's favourite spiritual sons was a celebrated comedian. He said, one day: "Padre Pio loved to tell jokes and he was even better at that than I am! He was good on repartee and made quick, funny remarks, like a great actor." And Campanini should know! A well-known journalist wrote: Padre Pio was a great talker, full of life and brilliant. Up against the wall, he was capable of the most extraordinary rhetoric to extricate himself. As if that were not enough he could disconcert people by saying something which really sounded bizarre and by making ironic remarks which upset their conclusions. As a good impersonator, he was appreciated even by those who generally could not stand this kind of thing! Above all, his rare sense of humour was evident to everyone." (See: L. Bedeschi — *His humour through fifty years as a priest.*)

Needless to say, Padre Pio's humour always had a meaning and he used it to advantage in his priestly ministry. He told many funny stories, but I present here just a few to give an idea of his kind of humour.

A recruit prepares for the King's visit

A sergeant was preparing a recruit for the king's visit to the barracks. He gave the young man these model questions and answers to learn by heart.

Question: How old are you?

Answer: Twenty-two.

Question: How many years of service do you have?

Answer: Two.

Question: Who would you serve most willingly, king or country?

Answer: One as much as the other, Your Majesty!

The king arrived but, unfortunately, he did not ask the questions in the order learned by the recruit. This is what happened!

Question: How many years of service do you have?

Answer: Twenty-two.

Question: How old are you?

Answer: Two.

The king became impatient and shouted at him: "Who is the bigger idiot here, you or me?"

"One as much as the other, Your Majesty!" the recruit replied.

Padre Pio laughs during a sermon

One of Padre Pio's confrères had seen him laugh during a sermon. Later, when they were together, he asked him why he had laughed during a sermon on death. Padre Pio replied in a Neapolitan dialect:

"What could I do about it? I couldn't help it! Some preachers would make you laugh at anything, even when they're talking about death!"

Padre Pio is not afraid of lightning

One of Padre Pio's Brothers was in the corridor with him during a violent thunderstorm. The lightning-flashes got nearer and nearer. Terrified, he turned to Padre Pio and said that they could be struck by lightning because they were standing near the electrical power panel. He added: "Father, we should, at least, move away from the panel. Yesterday, ten people were killed by lightning!" Padre Pio replied: "Then we don't need to be afraid. There are only two of us!"

Padre Pio for 20¢!

Padre Pio told this anecdote, one day, to some of his friends. It happened in 1922-23, when news got around that he had the stigmata. A photographer, who wanted to take advantage of this situation right away, took some photographs of Padre Pio and, although they were not very good, he had copies made and gave them to a boy to sell for 20¢ each. This boy was selling them a bit too near the monastery when Padre Pio heard him. "You riff-raff!" he yelled in a menacing voice, "I'll teach you to sell me for only 20¢!" The terrified boy ran off.

Padre Pio turned to his friends and said: "They could have sold me for a bit more than that!"

"Go, tell Professor Lunedei..."

Carlo Campanini, the comedian, tells of a friend, who was under the care of a renowned professor of medicine in Florence. He told the doctor that he was going to San Giovanni Rotondo to see Padre Pio. The professor exclaimed "What? You are going to see that hysteric? Scientifically speaking, that is what he is. By thinking so much and so often of Jesus Crucified he created the stigmata in his own body!"

The man did not allow himself to be swayed by these words. He went to Padre Pio for confession, then told him what the doctor had said. Padre Pio replied: "When you see your professor, ask him to think intensely and often of an ox, and see if he grows horns!"

A visit from the President of the Republic

The President of the Republic, Antonio Segni, came one day to visit Padre Pio. In presenting his entourage he introduced one of them as Deputy Russo. When he heard the word Russo (Russian) he asked: "Why have you brought me only one (Russian)? Bring many more to me!"

"With your kind of head, it would be difficult to sin!"

There was a woman, a kind of "femme fatale" in her young days, who had become a mere shadow of her former self. The years had taken their toll and she had become rather ugly.

She reflected on the vanity of human things and felt the need to go after more lasting values. So, she decided to go to Padre Pio for confession.

To get to him she had to register and wait her turn. This woman was not put off by the wait. She wanted to be sure of seeing Padre Pio, so she registered twice! She waited her turn patiently and, when it came, went to confession.

The next day, her second turn came up but, when Padre Pio saw her, he said: "You went to confession yesterday. What else do you want from me?" "But," the woman said, "since yesterday I might very well have sinned again!" "Nonsense," he said. "With a head like yours it would be difficult to sin!"

A humorous meeting

Two comedians went to see Padre Pio, one day. When Padre Pio saw them in the corridor he said: "Just look at those faces!" The man who introduced them said: "Father, these actors have decided to stop working with their legs and start working with their heads." Padre Pio replied quickly: "They should do that! The important thing is that they get it right!" When leaving them, he said: "Keep on being a disgrace. When all is said and done, you have never done anything to be proud of. Change that or I will throw you out!"

"Go ahead! This is your chance!"

Father Constantino Capobianco tells that he was becoming more and more hard of hearing until he could not hear at all. This was very humiliating for him. To help him, the Superior bought a hearing aid, which helped greatly.

One day in the course of a conversation, Padre Pio asked him how much he could hear without the aid. Father Constantino told him he could not hear at all. Padre Pio asked him to turn off his hearing aid for a few moments, then called out to the other friars: "Go ahead, boys! This is your chance to say what you want about Father Constantino!"

"So, who is to blame?"

Father Carmelo da Sessano was Guardian of the monastery when an order came from Rome authorizing a television crew to film a day in the life of Padre Pio. He resigned himself to this because the Superior asked him to let them do it and he thought it would not last very long.

When he came down from his cell to say Mass he was confronted by the film crew who went to work. He then went to the chapel of St. Francis where he celebrated Mass at this time. The noise of the camera disturbed him and he suddenly turned round and said: "Either you stop or I stop! I will go away and will not say Mass!"

They had to postpone the filming but started again afterwards, doing the best they could to catch other features of Padre Pio's day. He cooperated as little as he could and tried to limit the filming as much as possible. When it was finished at last, the Superior came to him and asked if he would see the crew who wanted to thank him and ask his blessing. He agreed and received the technicians who apologized for having disturbed him. However, they pointed out to him that it was not their fault, as they had their orders.

Padre Pio said to them goodnaturedly: "You had your orders, so it is not your fault. Father Guardian had his orders, so it is not his fault. The Superiors of the Province had their orders, so it is not their fault. The Major Superiors had their orders, so it is not their fault. Well, then, whose fault is it?"

"What do you want for a blessing? A pail of water over your head?"

Grazia, a young woman of twenty-nine, who lived nearby, often frequented the little church in the monastery at San Giovanni Rotondo. She had been blind since birth. Padre Pio asked her, one day, if she would like to see. Grazia answered that she would like to see if it would not cause her to sin. The priest told her she would be cured of her blindness and sent her to Doctor Durante, an excellent eye surgeon in Bari.

When he examined the blind girl, the specialist realized there was nothing to be done for her. He advised her to go back to Padre Pio and ask for a miracle. But the doctor's wife who was present pointed out that if Padre Pio had sent him this patient, it was because he knew something could be done. Why not try? The surgeon was persuaded to do the operation.

He operated first on one eye and Grazia's sight was restored. Then he did the other and she was able to see with both eyes. He was astonished and could not find any reasonable explanation! The girl could see.

As soon as she got back to San Giovanni Rotondo, Grazia went to thank Padre Pio. She threw herself at the feet of the priest she was seeing for the first time and told him of her joy, her admiration and her gratitude. Padre Pio stood still and looked at her, smiling. Grazia then asked for his blessing and he traced the Sign of the Cross over her. But Grazia continued to cry out: "Bless me, Father! Bless me!" She expected him to take her by the hand as he had done when she was blind. Finally, Padre Pio said to her: "What do you want for a blessing? A pail of water over your head?"

"They sing while I suffer!"

A companion of Padre Pio, who wanted to give him some comfort during the many illnesses he had to endure, told him one day that the people were concerned for his health and were praying for him. Padre Pio said: "That's right! They sing and I suffer. They are like the rooster who sings while the hen suffers laying an egg."

CONCLUSION

We are left to wonder at the variety and abundance of Padre Pio's charisms! So many gifts in one person! What is there to say about this? Aside from the unfathomable mystery of God, who calls his creatures to life and involves them in his universal plan by giving them a mission and means to accomplish it, we could also say that there is a "style" which governs the way the divine relates to souls. When someone is given to God totally and completely, God generously endows that person with a staggering variety of gifts which leave us speechless. I am tempted to say that, in Padre Pio's case, God enjoyed intervening in the most original and unexpected ways.

Padre Pio, as all his biographers show, had consecrated himself to God from childhood in a total and irrevocable way. And despite all his lengthy struggles against man and the devil, he remained faithful to this gift of himself to God. It is hardly surprising that God showered him with such graces.

There is a lesson here for us. To trust in God and abandon ourselves to him through all the events of life is to attain happiness, if we look at life with the eyes of faith. It is through faith that we come to an understanding of the real meaning of life, as it unfolds here on earth, and in its eternal perspective.

Printed in Canada — Imprimé au Canada

METROLITHO inc. SHERBROOKE